DEAR WHITE WOMAN,

Please Come Home

KIMBERLEE YOLANDA WILLIAMS

ELEPHANT
ROOM
PRESS

Elephant Room Press
Cambridge, MA

Cover design: Brad Norr, Brad Norr Design
Page design: Ebony Rose, Ignited Ink 717

Non-Fiction / Self-Help / Diversity & Inclusion

Kimberlee is available for keynotes, panels, book talks, and workshops.
Visit engagingacrossdifference.com to learn more and book Kimberlee.

Discounts for bulk purchases of 25 books or more are available.
Visit kimberleeyolandawilliams.square.site
to learn more and place an order.

Library of Congress Control Number: 2022931011

ISBN, print: 978-0-9913313-2-1
ISBN, ebook: 978-0-9913313-3-8

Printed in the United States of America

Dedication

This book is dedicated to all of my sistas whose stories fill these pages and to the white women who need to be taught and reminded that we are family.

Advance Praise

In her speculative epistolary memoir, Kimberlee Yolanda Williams cleverly imagines that white women are lost sisters who want to be found and brought back into community with Black women. Told through precise, relatable vignettes from daily life, Williams depicts the insult of microaggressions while presuming that white women want to be and do better. With equal force, Williams reckons with our divided times and beckons the way to a more united future. A compelling read for white and Black women alike. **Julie Lythcott-Haims**, speaker, activist, New York Times bestselling author

Through a series of deeply personal letters, Kimberlee Williams takes an innovative approach to antiracist struggle, powerfully connecting head and heart as she instructs with clarity and compassion. Not willing to give up hope for our collective liberation, Williams offers a guiding light as she calls white women home. May we find our way! **Robin DiAngelo**, PhD. Author of White Fragility and Nice Racism

Dear White Woman, Please Come Home caused us to pause for a moment and ask ourselves, with all these experiences, why would Williams still want us to be her sisters? Yet, she offers a beautiful and generous invitation for white women to see ourselves in her stories and reflect on the harm we cause in our everyday interactions with Black women. Deceptively subtle, we found ourselves engrossed in each story about "another" white woman. When we read the provocative questions she asks after each encounter, we realized that white woman was us! This is a much-needed book for all white women to read and reflect on how we can more authentically be in loving relationships with our sisters of color and reclaim our own joy when we come home. **Ilsa Marie Govan and Tilman Smith**, Co-Authors of What's Up with White Women: Unpacking Sexism and White Privilege in Pursuit of Racial Justice

In a series of heartfelt letters, Kimberlee Williams reaches out to the sister she knew in childhood — the one who shares her values and humanity, who is her friend and co-conspirator first...and white second — to bring her home to their friendship. Every woman Kimberlee meets on her search might be this long-lost sister, but whether the woman she's encountered has demanded her seat on the bus, ignored her in a meeting, cut in front of her in line or assumed she didn't have good enough credit to get a mortgage, each of them proves to be unprepared for sisterhood with Black and Brown women. It took me a few letters to get into the groove of the structure and storytelling style, but once in, I was completely hooked and just wanted more. I've read at least a dozen books that explain implicit bias and microaggressions, but Kim's clear, simple letters to the white woman she wants back in her life make these concepts crystal clear and undeniable. In the most subtle way imaginable, Kimberlee Williams manages to slam home to every reader what a microaggression is, when you are committing one, and how to be a true friend through empathy, care and allyship. This is a work of pure artistry and a catalyst for real connection. **Valerie Alexander**, keynote speaker, Author of How Women Can Succeed in the Workplace (Despite Having "Female Brains")

In Kimberlee Williams' Dear White Woman, Please Come Home, she captured her audience (me, a woman of color) by highlighting the racial divide between Black and white women (Sistas). She aptly describes the daunting experience to be Black and wanting to be accepted when acceptance means you have to be white. I am in awe of Williams stepping out and telling us we are "trapped so deep in our insulated identity lens" that we fail to look up to see for one second that we are Sistas. Thank you Kimberlee! **Varetta Mayes**, Board Leadership, The Flourish Collective

Kimberlee Williams' driving desire in Dear White Woman, Please Come Home is to heal and restore. She is on a hopeful, though at times discouraging, journey to reconnect with her true white sisters that she is convinced are out there. I was moved as a white reader to understand her depth of love for unity and wholeness in relationships across the Black/white divide. Yet, this book is anything but a mushy love story. Williams is gentle, but does not coddle. She expresses her hurt, anger, exhaustion and deep disappointment when she is rebuffed and overlooked time and time again. She calls white women to account, to look at their biases and instinctual actions and gives us questions at the end of each letter to reflect on how we've been complicit. I have read many books about race and reconciliation, but this style of writing personal letters helped me better understand an individual's pain and longing. It cuts to the core when she asks me to use my white privilege to 'lighten [her] load', to not remain silent, and to not miss opportunities to build a bridge. As much as this book helps me understand Blackness, it also helps me come face-to-face with my whiteness. This is a book I'll be handing out often! **Emily Nelson**, Executive Director, The Flourish Collective

Contents

Foreword

A few years back, Kimberlee and I sat at a conference lunch table, laughing over our shared disappointment in the day's "salad" offering – a lonely plate of iceberg lettuce. Amidst the joy of running into one another and the levity of the salad laugh, she mentioned to me a book she'd started writing. "It's a collection of letters, from me to white women," she explained. "Well actually, a white woman," she clarified. "Here, I'll read you one."

Somewhere around word ten, as I crunched my flavorless lettuce, I felt my eyes well up. I understood that she was trying, in a way I'd never seen attempted, to tap into white women's longing to be connected to intimate sisterhood beyond racial borders. As a white woman, my own longing sprung to the surface with a rawness I'd never felt before. Alongside it came a sickening pang, a thud of a reminder of the devastating role we white women have played in our centuries-old pattern of stepping on Black and brown women to preserve and advance our own interests while exploiting our sisters of color to maintain and enhance our physical and emotional comfort. That Kimberlee, despite this history, had summoned the grace to throw white women a lifeline in an effort to find one another anew filled me with a sense of wanting, no, *needing*, to back her up. "Would you ever consider using my imprint to publish this?" I asked. Without hesitation, she answered, "Let's do it." And here we are.

Eager to test my theory that Kimberlee's approach touched on something raw and new, I asked if I could share the letter she'd read to me with a few white women friends. Sure enough, they reacted as I had, with a visceral tear-up. "I didn't know any Black women had any interest in being friends with me," one said. I felt as if a family secret had been revealed.

Dear White Woman, Please Come Home is an invitation for white women longing for authentic friendship with Black and brown women, the kind of friendship with no place for secrets, the kind of relationship where truth-telling is welcome, even when it hurts. This invitation is not for the faint of heart, however; it comes with a make-or-break challenge: *We don't want you to come home until you're ready. Can we count on you to do that?* Her end-of-chapter questions give us the homework we white women need to start or deepen that process.

I especially appreciate Kimberlee's use of letters to a singular "missing white sister." White women, that's us! All of us. So indoctrinated in the myth of individualism, we too often forget to see ourselves as part of a group, as sisters. Kimberlee invites us to change that, to shift our hearts and minds from a me mode to an us mode as we consider the impact our distance, complacency, silence, perceived superiority, and controlling tendencies have on our Black and brown sisters.

May this book serve as an affirmation for women of color, whether or not you're still rooting for us white women to pull through. Kimberlee's stories center the Black brilliance, Black joy, and day-to-day ups and downs that are the context in which white women's predictable patterns of slighting, stepping on, misunderstanding, and looking through our sisters of color so abruptly and painfully land.

As a white woman, it has taken me a long time to appreciate the immense risk it takes for a person of color, gender aside, to share his/her/their truth with us white people. We have a long track record of denying (really? that doesn't sound right), minimizing (just ignore her), nitpicking (well what time of night was it?), judging (you are so sensitive!), and challenging (just let me play devil's advocate for a minute) the experiences of our brothers and sisters of color. We've done an exquisite job of sending signals that we don't care (all you ever talk about is race!). We can be disappointing, exhausting, and rage-inducing.

Kimberlee's attempt to penetrate this white wall with the vulnerability of painful personal memories, is nothing short of a monumental leap of faith. With this in mind, I urge all white women to remind yourselves and one another that these stories are gifts to be treasured, not nitpicked, or judged, or minimized, or challenged, or denied.

Every letter is based in real-life events she or one of her sisters of color has experienced with a white woman just like me, or you. Let's use them to know better so we can do better.

I feel in Kimberlee's approach a rare ability to meet us white women where we are, and then give us a push. For some this will feel like a nudge, for others a shove. Either way, let the momentum move you. Welcome her challenge to figure out what's expected of us. Lean into the effort she's made to help us help ourselves so we can show up authentically and consistently for our sisters of color. Kimberlee's hours and years of leading workshops to help white women better understand ourselves and our role in white supremacy feel both like a love song to sisterhood and a backbreaking labor of love. My hope is that white women will respond to her call with courage and vigor, and that Black and brown women will feel seen and centered in her work, ultimately able to exhale a bit as we white women learn how to share the burden of racism.

Can you imagine what could be possible if women

across racial, class, and other socially constructed borders could unite in the struggle to create organizations and societies where family, food, shelter, and wellbeing were centered? Where basic human rights were treasured priorities as opposed to resented obligations? The world needs our loving care, and we--we women--we need each other. First though, we need to understand the snares that trip us up.

White women, I invite you to make yourself a cup of tea, settle in with a notepad, read with an open heart and mind, and answer Kimberlee's end-of-chapter questions with all the thoughtful honesty you can muster. Gather your women friends and family and wonder together how different your life and our world could be if we could drop the superior/inferior roles handed to us and create something altogether new.

Women of color, I truly hope you have a white sister or two who you still believe in, and that this book could be your nudge to them.

For all of us, may those of us looking for one

another find the sisters we want and need. And from there, may we find the courage and endurance to hang together long enough to discover the possibilities and to change the narrative.

Debby Irving

1
From My Heart to Your Hands

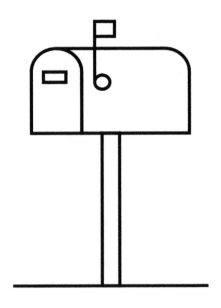

Dear White Woman,

I think you're out there looking for me. I know I'm looking for you. I tried to deny it for a long time. It just hurt too much to look and look for you and feel like you couldn't see me, like you looked right through me.

That workshop is where it all changed. Sitting in a session designed for Black women and white women to connect, communicate, and heal generations of brokenness, distrust, and unforgiveness, I heard this phrase repeatedly from every white woman who spoke: "I didn't know." I must admit that by the third time I heard a white woman say she didn't know how Black women felt, I started to doubt the level of honesty in the room. After the workshop, I went home questioning how they could possibly know if we as women of color had been trained to withhold the truth from them—if the real, raw, unfiltered truth was something we had been taught not to share for fear of fragility, retaliation, being ostracized, etc. It was then that I decided I would write this book, and in it, to tell the truth.

This book is written on behalf of the women of color in my family, my circle of friends, my colleagues, and the women of color existing throughout communities all over this country and the world. Now, please know that Black and brown people are not a monolith, so I do not speak for all of us. And, while I am unable to promise that all of us will agree with the words written here, I can tell you that I have met way too many women who do feel this way. These women's stories have inspired this book, and their voices are included in my quest for racial healing.

While many of my sistas* have given up on finding you, I have not. I continue to search for you each day and to look for signs of your return. I truly believe that I will find you, and we will reconnect like the sisters we were meant to be. I dream of seeing you, embracing you, and laughing or crying at all that we've missed since we were separated.

Now, a little about my why. This is what keeps me going; it's the belief that hundreds of years of silence, disrespect, and disconnection were part of a system handed to us instead of one that we created. We have participated in and allowed this separation in order to survive, but I'm not sure it's what either of us ever really wanted. We learned to suppress the desire to connect beyond the borders established for us. We learned to turn away from each other when our eyes met. You even learned to ignore my pain, no matter how great. But that's not you, sis. I have to believe that. That's why I look forward to the day when we will embrace one another.

While I know that the sister bond is one that can be filled with ups and downs and may even feel like a new concept to you, I still believe in it. I still believe in you. I still believe in us.

Now listen. My letters may make you laugh, cry, and even question your sanity, but they will consistently fill you with truth and love. They come from my soul and have landed in your hands because you are also searching for me.

Missing you,

Your sista

P.S. With the distance between us, you may have forgotten our native tongue and be confused with some of the language used in this book. To make things easier for you, I have defined some of these words at the end of each letter starting with the word sista.

*<u>Sista</u> – a term used among Black women for Black women. These letters are written by a Black woman on behalf of women of color to white women, our sisters. Please don't ever refer to yourself as a sista. This title refers to a deep connection that in my experience most white women don't feel for one another—a soul-level connection. If you are questioning what that means or feels like, you probably don't experience it. Because the smile I'm wearing right now as I write this just thinking about the bond I share with all of my sistas is not something that can be put into words.

Even if a Black woman "gifts" you this term, tread softly when trying to use it around other Black women. Your closeness with a select few sistas does not instinctively transfer to fondness from all of us. *Just my opinion, though.*

2
Let's Clear
This Up

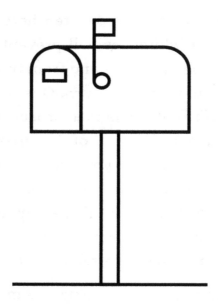

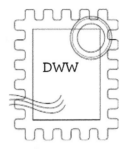

Dear White Woman,

Before I share the long journey of this search with you, I just want to clear some things up.

First, no matter how far-fetched these stories seem, they are all grounded in truth and told through the lens of imaginative nonfiction. So when you get to a place of doubt, come back to this letter, and reread these words.

This next point must be written here because I fear that your whiteness will prevent you from receiving these messages and from truly hearing my heart's call for your return. One of the major tenets of white culture is to approach everything from a head-space instead of a heart-space. So I can already see some of you questioning the idea or nature of this sister relationship. Was this person *actually* taken? Is this person *me*? Is this your *real* sister? Is she your *half* sibling? And so on and so forth down the rabbit hole.

Both of my parents are African American and

did not birth, foster, or adopt any white children. The relationship of sisterhood between us is one that Black women innately share. Walking down a sidewalk, a comment like, "Nice dress, Sis" is completely normal. It's to say "I see you, and I'm here for you if you should ever need me. I am your protector, your supporter, and your friend on our best day. On our worst day, I am your fiercest competitor and will stop at nothing to destroy you if we are fighting for a seat at the table where they only have room for one of us. I am all of these things and none of them on any given day. I am your sista."

So, I want you to dig deep and to suspend your attachment to practicality and realism and to come with me on this fluid and non-linear journey of the heart.

With love,

Your Sista

3
It's Your Face on the Milk Carton

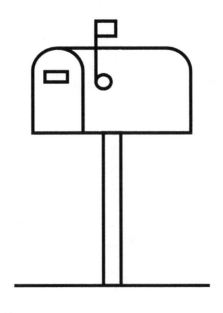

Dear White Woman,

I still remember the day you were taken away from us. I remember it like it was yesterday. When I think of it, I tear up, and I long to see you, to hold you, to laugh with you, and to cry with you. I want to hear every detail of what happened that day. I'd like to know who it was that convinced you that we weren't family. Who took you? Who changed you? Who erased your memory of who I am in your life? Who taught you to see me the way you do? To speak to me in such strange ways? To look down on the way we lived? Who convinced you that we were competition instead of compassion, separation instead of support, foe instead of friend? Who filled your heart with these lies?

I remember this day was just like any other. We arrived at school; we went to our classes and met up on the playground like we always did. You told me about the first half of your day, and I told you about mine. We played on different playground equipment, and you always defended me when kids made fun of me because I was too chubby to use the monkey bars, the jungle gym, or the see-saw. My favorite was the swings (although it was difficult to get on considering I was the shortest in my class) and it eventually became yours too, because it was the one thing on the playground we could do together. We went back to class for the second half of the day, and I waited for you in front of our bus stop like I always did. Mr. Brooks, the bus driver, yelled for me to get on, and I told him I was waiting for my sister. He yelled and yelled, threatening to leave us both, and I mustered up all the courage and screamed back, "No! I'm waiting for my sister just like Ma* taught us to do!" Mr. Brooks pulled off, and I waited. I waited for you, and I waited for you, and I waited for you.

The principal and a few other teachers came out and noticed I had not boarded the bus and was still there. She yelled at me too. "Kim, now why on earth would you miss your bus? You know your mom works way too hard to have to come up here to pick you up like this! Did your sister leave without you?"

How could she even ask me something like that? You would never have gotten on the bus and not checked to make sure that I was there! Right? Right! You would have never left me! Right?

Mrs. Cunningham took me into her office to call Mom. My mother was mad, and she yelled at me about us missing the bus. When she finally came up for air, I explained that I did what she always told me to do: I waited for you, but you never came. Mom and Dad came up to the school, and the police were waiting with me. There were so many of them. So many officers, so many neighbors, so many questions, and crawling down my face, so many tears. I had no idea what was going on, but I knew it was bad. I knew it was wrong. I knew our lives would somehow be different from that moment on.

You were gone. Never to return or to be seen again.

I had lost my sister.

Heartbroken,

Your Sista

*<u>Ma</u> – the word that my siblings and I used to call for, address, or refer to my mother. We also called her Mom. We continue to use these interchangeably.

Pause, Reflect, & Discuss

- What did you feel reading the story of the sister's disappearance?

- What part of the story seemed inconceivable to you?

- What do you hope to learn as you move to the next page?

4
The King's
English

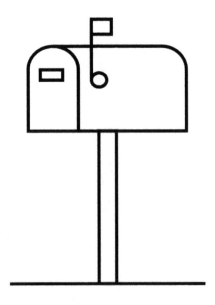

Dear White Woman,

Hey, sis. It is in a somber mood that I write this letter to you. Many years have passed since you were taken away from our family, and today we officially reopened the missing person's case to find you. We submitted a new police report, and we started putting up posters anywhere we could. The only reason we reopened the case is because all we ever did was sit around talking about you and how we wish you were here. And here's the thing: each story always finished with a "maybe she's still out there" tone.

We had to work with one of those age progression artists to come up with what you would look like today, and it's almost creepy to see it. To stare into your eyes and, yet, not feel your presence, and to see your smile and not be able to feel the warmth behind it was unusual, to say the least. You have to know we are doing everything in our power to find you and that we will never give up.

Today, as I was hanging up a missing person's poster, a woman came up behind me to ask questions. I felt motivated and encouraged that someone noticed the poster and wanted to ask me questions about you, so I stopped to engage in conversation with her. Once she began asking about you, I relaxed and let my guard down. You know how Ma taught us to keep our guard up, especially around white people, but she really and truly was interested in finding out more information about you and your case with the police department.

Then her questions seemed to shift to being more about the grammar used on the poster. She asked why there weren't enough commas, and why slang had been used, and why certain words weren't capitalized, and why the word "and" was used so much.

Sis! Oh my God! You and I both know Mom and Dad taught us to use the King's English when we needed to be accepted and tolerated by white people in white spaces to avoid their judgment. Dad even studied the dictionary for fun! So I turned to her and I said, "With two degrees on my mantel, I am certainly able to navigate the complexities and nuances of the English language in order to mitigate any preconceived notions about my education, identity, and value. However, when I am communicating with my family, I am allowed to chill and just be me. This is called code switching. This poster is for my sister, my family, and my friends. So it was written in my native tongue. You do know that African American Vernacular English is being recognized as a dialect of the English language, don't you?"

And, with that, I walked away.

The thing is, sis, had she said she was the chair of some missing persons committee who specialized in making missing persons posters more inviting by using certain graphics or phrases, I might have been open to her feedback. However, she wasn't a chair of any committee; she was just another white person judging my work.

Listen. All of these letters will be written in my "at-home voice" because they are written to you, my sister. I will not be code switching for the comfort of others, sis. This matter is too close to home and to the heart for me to be wasting my time code switching.

Ugh,

Your Sista

Pause, Reflect, & Discuss

- Do you recognize the microaggression in the letter? Do you know what a microaggression is? No, I won't be explaining it. This is a good time to look it up and to discuss it with others in the group, or in your family, or your friends, or your colleagues. (Those who identify as white, of course.)

- Have you ever missed what someone (especially a person of color) was saying because your mind automatically judged their "misuse" of grammar, misplacement of commas, or word choice? How has that impacted your relationships with people of color? How does this impact your relationships with other white people?

- Where does this knee-jerk reaction to the use of AAVE grammar and word choice come from? (Do you know what AAVE is? Hint: Look it up!)

5
Your Lips Must Be Numb

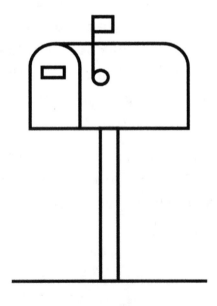

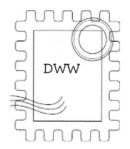

DWW

Dear White Woman,

I'm thinking back to the first time I thought we found you. We actually crossed paths in the produce section, and our eyes met. I was certain it was you, but you shared a brief smile and kept it moving. As you turned and walked away, I thought to yell, "Well, good morning to you too!" but I let it go and continued shopping.

Passing through the aisles, I thought about you and how it could be possible that you did not recognize me, your sista. Thankfully, I got another chance to share a "hello" since we ended up in the same checkout line. You responded with the tiniest smile and looked down at your coupons. I thought for sure we'd start chatting about how great the weather was, or how long the line was...but nothing.

As I finished up my transaction, the cashier asked for my identification even though the back of my credit card was signed. I looked at you with shock in my eyes, knowing that my sister would intervene and ask the cashier why she needed to see my ID, but you looked away and pretended not to hear. Remember how Ma always told you that because you were born with white skin that other white people would likely listen to you over your Black and brown siblings? I remember that she told you how she expected you to be a good ally to me, the same way she told us we'd both need to be good allies to our older sister who was born with learning differences. Well, this was your chance to use your white-skinned privilege to make a difference, to lighten the load that folks of color are carrying, to lighten my load, sis, but you didn't. It was almost as if you had lost the feeling in your lips, and that's why you didn't say anything. I hung around to see if the cashier also wanted to see your ID, but just like I'd imagined, she didn't. It was then that I thought *maybe that isn't her*. But maybe you didn't know what lightening my load looked like in this particular situation, because you *always* knew growing up. Maybe you were too timid to speak to the cashier. All I needed you to do was to address me, your sista, in front of the cashier and say something like, "Absolutely not. I never show my ID here, and neither will you." That would have been enough.

Sadly, these moments come up everywhere you look for them. Literally everywhere. But they are generally missed opportunities if you aren't looking for them.

I'll tell you, that day I walked away disappointed and disturbed, hurt and hopeless, wondering if I'd ever find you, the real you. I know you're out there. I won't give up! I can't! I will continue searching for you, and I'll recognize you after all these years because you won't be able to turn away from me and be satisfied with a smile as a way to acknowledge my humanity.

Still searching,

Your Sista

Pause, Reflect, & Discuss

- Can you think of a time where you witnessed something you knew in your gut wasn't fair based on race? What did you do? If you could relive that moment, how might it be different?

- Is this the first time you've heard that being a white person makes it much more likely that a white person will listen to you over your Black and brown siblings?

- What might it cost your relationships with your colleagues, classmates, friends, and neighbors of color if you choose not to speak up?

6
Where's That Ding?!

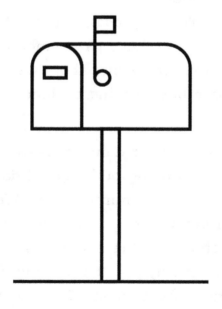

Dear White Woman,

I woke up to the sunrise on my face and smiled at the thought of feeling that same warmth when we finally get the chance to reconnect. After showering and reflecting on all that we've lost as the years have passed us by, I mapped out my route for locating you today. Just as I sipped my warm tea looking out over the water, I watched the storm clouds roll in and felt discouraged. *Maybe I shouldn't go out today,* I thought, *'cause she probably isn't there.* Then, I remembered how we used to say that life wasn't about waiting for the storm to pass but learning to dance in the rain instead.

Do you remember our dance classes, sis? Yep, I remember Mom being our original dance coach and us hating every minute of it. We were up at 3:00 am practicing, and we were performing most weekends. I still remember when I actually fell in love with it, sis. It was long after you'd been separated from us, and I found dance to be healing—an escape, a sanctuary, a way out of all that I was feeling and thinking about. It was no longer about how flexible I was or how the lead role belonged to me. It was no longer about what I could give to audiences through dance. It became about what dance could give to me. Anyways, remembering all of this, I smiled, grabbed my umbrella, and headed for the door.

I anxiously waited for the elevator while rehearsing what I'd say to you: "Hi, I'm Kim." No! "Hi! I'm Kimberlee." No. Ugh! "Hi, do you remember me?" Too scary. Ugh! The bell for the elevator dinged and I got on. It stopped on the floor just before the parking garage and I looked up out of pure curiosity. Believe it or not, it was you! I hadn't even left my building, and yet there you were standing next to me in my own elevator! Our eyes met briefly, and all that I had rehearsed fell into that empty awkward space between us. So I mustered up a "Hi! The weather is nice today!" You looked away after smiling briefly. My heart sank as you pulled out your phone and scooted to the edge of the elevator as if I posed a threat to your safety. Traveling down just one floor seemed to be the longest ride of my life.

The bell dinged once again, and you hurried through the only partially opened doors. Was it not you? No, I am certain it was you! The curved lines near your mouth reminded me of how much we used to laugh together at little nothings that only we found funny. The slump in your shoulders showed just how long it has been since we last spoke because we always unloaded our burdens in our late-night chats before bedtime. Remember how we called them "heart-to-hearts"? Those chats filled me up on a soul level that few understand. It seemed that you were now carrying decades and maybe even centuries of our ancestors' trauma that you used to share with me, your sista. You know how being a part of the collective has always somehow made us the bearer of others' burdens like us and those who came before us—that tribal thing we share. But maybe your look is very similar to so many others like you. Members of your own tribe, huh? And... Maybe... Hmmm... Just maybe, it wasn't you after all.

But don't you worry! Tomorrow is a new day, and each moment brings renewed hope of finding you. Now, if you see me in an elevator tomorrow, a simple "good morning" would work. And watch your body language, too, 'cause you aren't *actually* afraid, are you? Oh, and I've got a trunk full of your favorite things, and I promise to bring some so that you recognize me and can start the healing process... To remember who you were. Who we were. Are. Right! Who we *are*.

Determined,

Your Sista

Pause, Reflect, & Discuss

- In what ways has your discomfort in the presence of those different from you manifested in physical ways like moving away from someone, throwing your hands up as if being held at gunpoint, or clutching your purse/bag/wallet? What happened? Did you identify your discomfort? Did you interrogate it or discuss it with anyone, or did you simply stuff it down and pretend it didn't happen?

- Have you ever responded to someone's greeting with a smile/head nod/grunt instead of using your words to respond? Describe this interaction and why you might think it is socially acceptable. How does this deter and discourage women of color from seeing you as an ally, a friend, or even a sister?

7
Unhoused for the Holidays

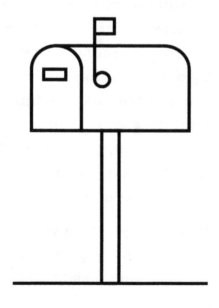

Dear White Woman,

Hey, sis.

I'm tired.

I'm so fucking tired!

I knew this search would be tough, but I never imagined how exhausting and draining it could be to reopen it. Being microaggressed* every day, all day, is what a student once described as "death by a thousand cuts." That's exactly what it feels like. To live the trauma of being "othered" day in and day out with comments and questions that are preventable with a quick Internet search makes me want to give up. Maybe I shouldn't even be looking for you, you know? The police did say you are now old enough to be living your own life—whatever that means.

Take for instance last year. I was a volunteer for one of the largest holiday parties I'd ever been to. The party was for unhoused families and their children. Every well-known politician was there, and even Santa and his wife made an appearance. There were rides, candy, presents, music, mascots, and so much more. There were also children from all over the city who were eager to get into this magical place set up just for them. As a volunteer, my job was to keep the flow of families headed in the right direction. So I stood on the sideline with all of the other volunteers, wearing my bright volunteer shirt, and helped to keep the line moving with cheers like "Welcome!" or "Merry Christmas!" and "Happy Holidays! Let's keep moving!" And then it happened. I thought I saw you helping direct families, too!

You had a clipboard but no volunteer shirt. *Maybe you were in charge of volunteers.* I knew it was you because you were really good at running events. I straightened my clothes and waited for an opportunity to speak to you. You started heading my way, and I got butterflies! *Is she coming my way or one of my fellow volunteer's? Wait, no, she's coming to me!* You got really close to me and said in a really loud voice, "Ma'am, I'm going to need you to keep moving!" And, just like that, I knew it wasn't you. My co-worker, an Asian American woman who was passionate about all things diversity, equity, and inclusion, saw what happened and silently mouthed to me, "I'm sorry, Kim."

What was it that made me look like I was also unhoused? I stood with the workers on the sidelines and made conversation. I wore the t-shirt like everyone else. I waved my arms and shouted all the rehearsed greetings to keep the flow of families moving and to get the children excited. So, what was it that made me look unhoused to this white woman? I looked around and realized that out of the thousands of people pouring into and standing around in this venue, I was the only Black volunteer in that part of the venue. That fact weighed on me like a ton of bricks. Had she simply asked, "Which housing agency are you here with?" I would have clarified my position for her. But the fact that she needed to question my presence at all enrages me. It felt like hearing, "Where are your slave papers?"

Today, I still wonder why she didn't just ask me what agency I was with or why she didn't ask anyone else around me why they were there. I question why it's always the presence of Black women that makes white women so uncomfortable.

And, yes, I'm still angry about it, sis. But I know it wasn't you.

My anger belongs with her.

Not you.

Needing to process,

Your Sista

*Microaggressed (in case you never looked it up like I told you to, sis) — to experience the intersection of someone's ignorance or implicit bias and your cultural norm. These often come in the form of seemingly innocent comments, questions, or actions.

Pause, Reflect, & Discuss

- Name a few examples of microaggressions you have committed. Search "microaggressions" to find some lists of common microaggressions if needed.

- What were the underlying biases and cultural norms?

- Name the steps you are taking to unlearn the implicit biases you shared in response to the last question.

- Have the women of color you've encountered felt safe enough to let you know when you've microaggressed them? If they haven't, what does that cost your relationship? Is it really as close as you thought it was?

8
It's Just Jam!

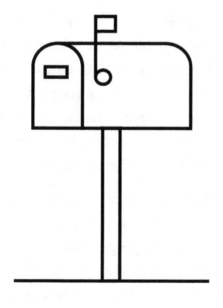

DWW

Dear White Woman,

I got home late from the mall last night and checked my voicemail messages as soon as I got in. I thought maybe someone had spotted you and contacted me with the details. After a few messages from family, clients, and friends, sure enough, some guy named Jim had seen my "Seeking My Lost Sister" flyer and told me that he runs into you weekly at the local recycling center. I went digging through my fridge and cabinets looking for every piece of plastic, metal, and glass I could possibly find! I came up with quite a few bags, and then the nerves hit me. "What should I wear? I mean, this is it! What should I say? Ah, it doesn't matter. She'll recognize me and do all the talking like she always does!"

After a restless night of tossing and turning, I loaded the car, fluffed my big hair once or twice, put on my cutest leggings that I knew you'd love (the black ones with the stars all over them), and headed out the door. I needed to get there a few minutes before you, so I could set up our perfect interaction. You know I wanted to stage the perfect choreography!

I arrived at the same time Jim was pulling up and got all of the recycling items unloaded. I positioned myself at the last set of bins to give you the space you'd need to process that you were indeed seeing your sista after all this time. And then, it happened!

Jim pointed out your car as you pulled in, and a smile of excitement and anticipation spread across both of our faces! You unloaded your car and headed our way. What a beautiful car you drove. Nothing fancy, but roomy enough for tons of recycling. I giggled to myself with nervousness, and my stomach started to ache like I was about to go on stage to perform before an audience. But I pretended to be cool and calm like you'd taught me when we were kids performing together.

As you entered, you gave Jim a big smile and greeted him with a friendly, "Good morning, Jim. All is well, yes?" Jim returned the greeting and winked at me. I stretched my neck to see past him and greeted you with a "Good morning!

How are you today?" You looked down at your recycling and began to sort things and muttered, "Fine, thanks." I panicked and rushed over to you to strike up a conversation and to recycle my things in the machines next to yours. I thought, How long's it been? But wait, something was different.

You had a look of disgust on your face as you noticed the jar of jam that I was recycling, as if you'd never tasted it and certainly wouldn't risk your health for a teaspoon of the poison. I dismissed your judgment and kept mentioning things from our youth in hopes you would remember me. I recounted stories of the park we walked to and the swings we'd rocked back and forth on. You only looked even more lost, as if this information was foreign to you. I turned to Jim with confusion settling in my eyes and disappointment in my fading smile. With a shrug of his shoulders, I knew Jim was mistaken, and he knew it too.

I was so disappointed that I grabbed the rest of my belongings and headed out the door, too embarrassed to tell you I had mistaken you for my long-lost sister. I knew it couldn't have been you. The real you would have remembered how much we loved that jam I had, and how much the swings were our favorite with the sun on our faces as we rose to the sky and the wind at our backs as we fell towards the earth. It simply could not have been you.

You didn't even notice my stylish leggings! They'd easily be your favorite!

Don't worry sis, I haven't given up. I won't. I simply will not. I have spoken with several private investigators, and we continue to post flyers all over the state spreading the news of your disappearance. Although I must confess that I secretly wish white women would take up this search to find you. That they would even notice your disappearance and then lead it. That they would be able to notice what happened at the recycling center, speak up about it, and then carry on the search. When I say speak up, I mean something like, "Hey! My nana loves that jam! Let me guess! You think there is high fructose corn syrup in it, right? No ma'am. All natural and low in sugar." And, just like that, it would have been a more pleasant experience. Questions and curiosity before judgment, please.

Probably wishful thinking, right?

Loving you from a distance,

Your Sista

Pause, Reflect, & Discuss

- Describe a time where your cultural norms have led to you consciously or subconsciously judge what someone eats. Did you comment on their food choices? Did your facial expression speak for you?

- In what other ways have you judged someone's life if their choices did not reflect white cultural norms? (For those looking for examples: unmarried and childless after 32 years of age, not taking yoga classes, not going for daily runs, purchasing a puppy instead of adopting one from a shelter, spending money on hair care, spending money on anything at all that you judge as unnecessary. Need I go on?) How might these judgments harm your relationships with women of color? How might they prevent women of color from ever trusting you?

9
Big Hair,
Don't Care

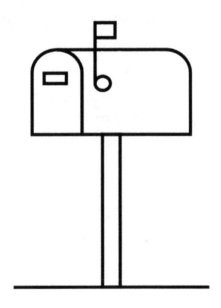

Dear White Woman,

I was in the mirror this morning pulling back one of my braids, and I realized my braids or my "big hair" might be confusing to you, since my hair was chemically straightened when you were taken from the family. So I'm sharing my hair journey with you today, sis, hoping that it will help you recognize me when you see me.

I remember being younger and having three things that controlled and maintained my tresses: the hot comb*, water, and Vaseline. Sometimes a combination of all three were used to tame my big and wild hair. You see, the goal was for our hair to be as close as we could get it to what white folks felt comfortable looking at. We were always on a mission to fit in with, to be accepted or tolerated by, or to assimilate to be like, white people.

Whiteness was literally the goal. While it was never stated, I look back now and understand it was indeed the standard. Otherwise, you'd stand out for all the wrong reasons.

Anyways, when the hot comb was not good enough, because our tight curls and coils would come back if our hair got even a little wet (swimming, sweating, showering, rain, and drizzle, etc.), we stepped up to the more aggressive and more permanent form of straightening: a relaxer. And, no, a perm did not make our hair curly. That's what happens to white folks' hair when it's permed. For Black people, it straightens our hair. While it didn't get super curly when it got wet, it still was a two-hour process (minimum) for me to go from wet hair to something presentable or acceptable in public.

I continued this process every four to six weeks for two very long decades. My roots were treated with chemicals to straighten the curly hair that had more recently grown out of my scalp. While the finished product was beautiful according to European standards, the pain of the chemicals burning my scalp or places along my hairline was undeniable and unlike anything you've known or felt. Imagine, we relax our coils to straighten them while you may have permed yours to add curls. Go figure.

This was all in an effort to be more white. Did I ever say that? No. Did I ever think that? No. I just wanted to be accepted. And that meant I wanted to be white. Everything white was accepted. Not only accepted, but normal, beautiful, perfect— the standard. So if I had to straighten my hair to fit in, and it became more manageable, then I was in.

Until...

One day, I sat in a salon chair in Dallas, Texas, and heard the words, "You have follicles where there is no hair growing out of your scalp, and this will only spread."

My whole world came crashing down.

My entire life was spent believing that my hair was my glory, and it was one of the main things that made women beautiful. And what made us even more beautiful was having hair like white women...as long and as straight as theirs.

Wanna know what she said next?

"Kim, you have to stop straightening your hair."

She might as well have said, "Kim, you have to stop being beautiful."

I began weeping. I thought natural hair was ugly. How could I not think that, when that's all I knew? I was taught to make fun of girls who couldn't find a strong enough chemical to straighten their curls. And I did.

I went home and I cried and cried. I couldn't eat. I couldn't sleep. And I couldn't stop crying.

This meant I would turn into one of the "ugly ones."

I worried, and I worried, and I cried.

Then, one day while waiting for an elevator, one of my sistas with beautiful locks talked to me about all the possibilities ahead of me if I'd let my natural hair grow out.

Suddenly, I felt hopeful. Still anxious, but at least now also hopeful.

You see, sis, the only option was to cut off my straightened hair and to let my natural hair grow out. This was a hard decision. And hard is an understatement. Knowing our hair seems to grow more slowly than white women, I was depressed that I'd be seen as "bald" for years.

Before I could even do the big chop*, I had to be seen by a dermatologist to determine just how bad the damage was to my scalp. She confirmed that it was progressively getting worse and would continue if not treated. So, for six months, I endured scalp injections to stop the balding. Painful! Needles were literally injected into my scalp! Ugh!

After the six months of injections, I went in for the big chop. The stylist cut my hair all the way down to a very mini afro. I was stunned. Stunned because I was still beautiful when she swung the chair around. Stunned because I didn't recognize my hair. Stunned because I didn't know how to love it, how to care for it, or where to even begin.

I tried wearing braids* to avoid having to learn how to love and care for my hair. I wanted what I saw as the easy way out. That didn't work for me given that I wasn't used to it, and the weight of the braids hurt my neck so badly. But I had paid too much money ($200) and sat in that chair for way too long (six hours) to take them out. So, I endured six weeks of neck pain and tension headaches.

That was beyond awful, so I eventually started watching videos to learn how to care for my hair. While I still didn't know how to love it, I began to embrace the journey of learning how.

The more I learned, the more I loved it.

I loved my hair.

I loved it in braids with my own hair.

I loved it in my big, huge afro.

I literally fell in love with my hair.

I fell in love with myself.

I love my Blackness.

And you know what? I love me just the way I am.

Just thought you should know,

Your Sista

Hotcomb (aka pressing comb) – a device invented by Madam C.J. Walker that is used on a stove where the comb is heated all the way up, blown on a little bit, and then used to straighten your hair from root to tip. It is often used in combination with grease/oil, so your hair is kinda fried. Your scalp and skin are often burned in this process. Not a formal definition. Just my take on it, as I have been through it many times.

The Big Chop – an event where someone goes to cut off all of their chemically processed hair to allow their natural hair to grow out. Yes, it is an event. This can be a very emotionally painful and/or even freeing process.

Pause, Reflect, & Discuss

- What sacrifices in your physical appearance have you made to be seen as beautiful? How have those sacrifices impacted your relationships?

- What have you done to support the Crown Act (if you're confused, look it up)?

- How might your ignorance about Black hair impact your relationships with women of color?

10
It's Always the
Same With
You

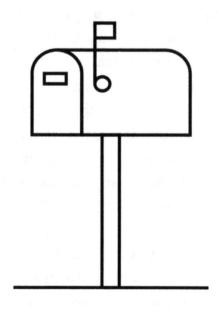

Dear White Woman,

Today I thought I'd throw caution to the wind and just embrace the little kid inside me. Not an actual baby, sis! I'm talking about the proverbial child who lives in each of us. Why judge myself for just wanting to have fun, right?

So our dog Kwinee (our Cavapoo--half Cavalier King Charles Spaniel and half mini poodle) and I headed over to the playground that sits in the center of our neighborhood, surrounded by a walking trail. I know you're wondering where that name came from because names always mean something to us in this community. Well, we took the K in Kim and my partner's nickname, Win (what many of my family members and friends call her, but her real name is Denise), and put them together to make Kwin. Of course, just like my first name and Win's last name, everyone spells it wrong, lol. They always want to write Quin. Anyways, while this trip was not really about running into you, the unthinkable and inconceivable did indeed happen.

You know I got there just as the sun was rising, so I wouldn't have to wait for a swing, and hoped it would be sacred and meditative alone time. You know me, sis. Anyways, I tied Kwinee to the pole and hopped on the first available swing. I rocked back and forth, pumping my legs until I reached a good enough height. Thankfully I wore my sunglasses, so the sun in my face was a yummy part of today's visit. I was so immersed in the giddy feeling of letting myself be a kid again that I barely noticed you enter the playground with a few of your friends. Back and forth, higher and higher, cool breeze, warm sunshine. Life just literally couldn't get any better than this. I had abandoned my detective role for just a few moments of carefree living.

Just as I rose to the sky for the millionth time, I heard giggles from somewhere and thought someone had come to join me in this moment of embracing the time we have on earth. I turned towards the sounds of laughter and thought I spotted you. No, it couldn't be. I'm not even searching right now, but could it be her? Nah, not possible, I thought. Besides, *what could be that funny?*

As I slowed my swing to nearly a stop, I heard a few whispers. "Can you believe her?" "She needs to be in the gym instead of on that swing," and lastly "What's she doing here scaring our neighbors and their children with that rat's nest on her head?" Ohhh, my big scary hair again, sis. My weight and my hair again. And again, and again, and again. Always the same story for me. I have always weighed more than my peers, and I have always had a lot of hair. However, after a few years of tending the garden that is my hair, like I told you, now it's even bigger. Had anyone in the group of friends spoken up and said that my body and my hair were none of their business, I might have felt seen and cared for in that moment.

Anyways, I untied Kwin and headed your way for a closer look, and you turned away, lifted your sunglasses and trotted off towards the walking trail to run with your friends. I stood there overtaken by the distance between us and the confusion that flooded my soul.

In that instant, I thought to myself, *It couldn't be*

you because you would never see me and say such hurtful things about me. Do you have children now? What about me and my hair was so scary for them? No, it couldn't have been you. But today's interaction on the playground that ushered in dark clouds over my sunshine was enough for me to head home and to give up. I got to the car, loaded Kwin inside, sat in the driver's seat, and screamed a gut-wrenching cry of frustration and surrender. For today, I had given up searching for you. I am wounded, sis. I need rest.

For now.

Disappointed and needing self-care,

Your Sista

Pause, Reflect, & Discuss

- Describe the last time you let your inner kid come out where alcohol or actual children weren't involved? Does this concept seem strange to you? Why or why not? How might this create distance between you and women of color?

- Share about a time when the body type/size/ shape or hairstyle of a woman of color made you uncomfortable, made you stare a bit too long, or brought up judgments.

11
She Ain't Welcome Here!

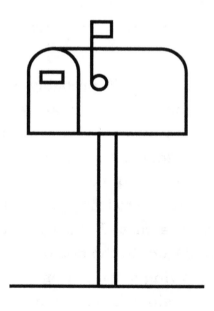

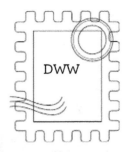

Dear White Woman,

Sis! I'm having a cheat day today! Well, not in a diet sort of way, lol. I mean I'm allowing myself to go to my favorite coffee shop downtown and to have my favorite hot drink. *Vanilla chai!* I know you must be wondering why vanilla chai would be a "cheat day" for me. So the truth is I'm not supposed to have caffeine because of my high blood pressure, but every so often I cannot resist it. It is so good and so calming for me. I literally love it!

Knowing you, you will probably worry about my blood pressure because you were always so caring. So, I was diagnosed during the week of Dad's funeral. *I know; I know.* This is too much to put in one letter, but of course my thoughts are racing around trying to bring you up to speed on everything you've missed. During that time, I felt really sick and went to the doctor; I was running a fever and blowing blood out of my nose. Turns out that I had a sinus infection and a double ear infection. On top of that, my blood pressure was in the "stroke zone." The stress of planning a funeral and processing Dad's death did not help any of the things ailing me. *Don't worry, we'll talk about Dad's passing in another letter, I promise.*

Anyways, they told me no caffeine! So every once in a while, I indulge in a warm and yummy vanilla chai.

This time, I was sitting in a corner of the coffee shop alone with my drink and my daydreams. While off in a field of lavender somewhere in my mind, I felt a tap on my shoulder, bursting my self-care bubble. It was one of my best friends dropping in for a quick coffee. It was so weird yet so amazing that we were there at the same time. It felt good to hug her and to hear about what was going on in her life. We sat together and laughed and sipped our drinks of choice.

Then, the conversation turned.

It went like this:

Friend: Sis, I heard you were reopening that case again. I know you ain't thinking about reopening it. *Are you?* Do you remember how much it hurt you the last time?

Me: Sis, please don't start. You know I feel called to do this. I can't rest unless I do.

Friend: A'ight, sis. But you know white women ain't checkn'* for you, for me, or for none of us.

Me: Sis! Yes they are! They just don't know that they are.

Friend: Fine. Let's say she does come home. Who is going to tell her not to bring all of the dirt and bad habits on the bottom of her shoes into our house? You gonna let her track all that mud in our home? Who is going to help her unlearn the tone that she speaks with? Who is going to teach her how offensive her very nature is? Not me! You gonna be responsible for all that? 'Cause we ain't gonna help you. I don't know why you just don't leave her out there to her own vices. She can keep her poison as long as she don't bring it this way. You gonna invite her home, and other folks will move out to avoid her.

Me: Sis!

Yup, that's how that conversation went.

Anyways, it's hard to believe that any of our sistas wouldn't be excited to search for you, but I guess it makes sense. It's been many years since any of us have even wanted to look for you. I feel so alone in this search sometimes and even think I may be making a mistake by asking you to come home. I just don't want you to feel isolated or even to unintentionally offend your family members when you return.

Conflicted,

Your Sista

*Check'n for — another way to say interested in, invested in, paying attention to, concerned for/ with, etc.

Pause, Reflect, & Discuss

- Did you think about your favorite warm drink while reading this? What is it?

- Are you aware of the science behind the disproportionate numbers of African Americans suffering from high blood pressure? Search "What you need to know about hypertension in African Americans" to learn more about its connection to racism. What messages have you gotten to explain this phenomenon?

- Name as many reasons as you can that a woman of color might not welcome you home. Would you even feel at home?

- What is it that my friend doesn't want to be responsible for teaching you? How might we begin? Would you be open to learning?

12
What's There to Sing About?

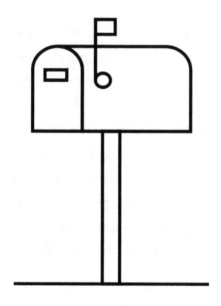

Dear White Woman,

So I'm so glad to finally get to sit down for a moment with my pen to write you another letter, 'cause it's been a while, sis. You are not gonna believe what happened to me today at work! Literally, like something you'd see on TV. I was the subject of a real-life intervention! My mouth is literally still hanging open, wondering how I didn't see it coming....

I got to work and went to settle my things in my office before knocking things off my To-Do List, and a group of my closest "friends"/colleagues came into the lounge to "get coffee." Each one looked genuinely concerned and sat down at the table where I was sipping on their stale-ass tea. Sis, you know I knew from coaching the clients in my practice what was getting ready to happen. An intervention. But I wasn't someone suffering from an addiction or some obsession! I was me!

They each began to say sentimental stuff like

"We're worried about you," or "You aren't getting enough sleep," or "If you pour any more out for her, you won't have anything left for you." Her? Her who? They couldn't possibly be talking about you!

I calmly listened without defensiveness just like I teach my clients to do. They suggested that I spend too many of my waking hours searching for you and that I needed to get out and do something fun. What they offered next as their idea of fun was tickets to the opera. Now you know I ain't never been to no opera! And I sure hadn't planned to start going now! But they had already purchased the tickets. So I put on my best dress, my shiniest earrings, my highest heels, fluffed my big natural hair, sucked it up, and went. Lawd, I still can't believe I agreed to go to the opera!

We pulled up in the middle of busy New York City streets right outside the theater. It was cold and rainy, but I was looking good, so I didn't mind strutting my stuff. Here I am, supposed to be taking a night off from searching for you and I'm still thinking about you and where you are! Does she like opera? Would she be here tonight? No. I never remember her mentioning the opera, and we certainly never went together. But maybe she changed and is here tonight. So in that moment, I decided to use tonight to my advantage without coming off too obsessive. I looked around and looked around, scanning each face, and nothing.

Right as we took our seats and waited for the show to begin, I heard a familiar laugh. It was loud, nerdy, and seemed like the person was stifling back a whole river of laughter that whatever was so funny merited. It sounded so similar to my own laugh, like I'd heard that type of self-control before, like I'd heard that laugh all through elementary school. Turning in that direction to see if the wave of laughter would hit me and my friends, I was floored! It was you who was laughing! The laugh was so recognizable to me because it was your laugh! You are the only person I know who would find something hilarious and not allow yourself to laugh as loud and as hard as you'd like. Of course, this would be different if we were at home in the comfort of our own community, but anyways....

Ohhhh, I started planning, honey! I figured out how I'd approach you but wanted to be careful not to scare you off. Hmmm... *I know! The bathroom at intermission!* Ugh, sis, I waited and waited while trying not to fall asleep during this show that everyone else found so captivating. Round of applause. Standing ovation. And, finally, the lights came on, and people herded themselves to the bathroom. I politely excused myself and headed that way too.

I got closer to you and after waiting in what seemed like the line to get into an amusement park, we ended up at the sink washing our hands next to each other. I heard you mutter something about appreciating true art and how much you'd been enjoying yourself. Once you took a break to reach for your paper towels, I dared to keep it simple and looked at your reflection in the mirror right into your eyes with a friendly, yet not too friendly, "Hello." You looked back at my reflection and said nothing. *Literally nothing!* I was so embarrassed that I took off out of that bathroom like lightning was sure to strike it at any minute! I walked as fast as I could back to my seat, steaming hotter than lava from a volcano.

How dare she not speak to me?! I'm her sista for God's sake! What the hell is going on here? All she had to say was, "Hi." That's it. I wasn't looking for a dissertation. Just a greeting!

Anyways, keeping my composure and not really wanting to fall asleep on the second half of the show, I made up some bullshit excuse about getting my period and caught a car service to the train station to head home. Yes, home, sis. It's the one place that so many of us Black folks feel the most safe. I just couldn't bear to face you, and I certainly couldn't prove my coworkers' suspicions correct by telling them what had happened.

I got home and cried into my pillow with anger, hurt, and so many questions. Like, who taught you not to speak when people speak to you? Like, why do you act afraid of me? Like, why do you stare at me when I enter public places? So many questions.

Whew, tomorrow is a new day. I will keep my search on the low*, but I will not give up until I find you, sis. I'm really hoping you are out there doing your work* and looking for me at the same time.

Discouraged yet determined,

Your Sista

On the low – a secret, being discreet about something.

Doing your work – a phrase often used by counselors, therapists, and even activists when it comes to diversity, equity, inclusion, and belonging. While it may seem that it means reading books, listening to podcasts, and donating money, it really means allowing people to hold you accountable so you can start unlearning behaviors and norms that are offensive and oppressive.

I can hear you saying, "Like what?" Let's start with that empty smile you give when someone says good morning/hello/good evening to you. Instead, make eye contact, smile, and return the greeting. That's doing the work. It means you actually need to open your mouth and let words come out. Can you do that, sis?

Pause, Reflect, & Discuss

- What art form do you appreciate and subconsciously believe everyone else should too? (Museums, art shows, art auctions, the ballet, the opera, etc.)

- What was your reaction the first time you realized almost everyone at those events looks like you? Or did you just find out while reading the question? Why aren't more people of color found at these events? Why are you at these events?

13
And You Think
We're Violent?

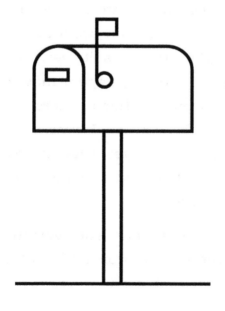

Dear White Woman,

It's late in the evening now, as I sit down to write to you. I just got back from my first, and probably my last, hockey game. After much coercing from my more-daring family members, I agreed to go in celebration of our younger brother's graduation from basic training for the United States Air Force.

It was after we pulled into the parking lot that I realized this was also an opportunity to search for you in a place that wasn't even on my radar to check. I mean after all, I spent most of my time growing up around other dancers in the studio or at church. Never had I ever seen a hockey practice, game, or player. I had no expectations for this game but had the highest hopes for spotting you there.

We walked into the arena, and everything seemed "normal," but what is "normal," really? And who gets to decide what "normal" is?

Anyways, we grabbed a few snacks from the concession stands and headed to our seats. The first thing I noticed was the cold. It was freezing in there! No wonder there was so much alcohol being passed around! People needed to warm up! 'Cause, who actually enjoys the taste of beer?! (Not me! But maybe they did.) As the seven of us paraded into our row, it was as if the ref called a timeout. Everyone stopped to stare at us. And then, the cold didn't seem so bad. I'll tell you the fans managed to be colder than the ice under the skates of those players.

We took our seats, and I immediately began to scan the faces in the crowd to look for you. Blonde? No, she definitely had dark hair as a kid. Not her. Red? No, unless the beauty supply store had a sale going on.... Oh! Wait! Dark hair! Medium tall! Beautiful eyes! There! It was you! I even saw the birthmark on your hand as you cheered for the teams. You turned around and caught me staring at you and looked the other way. But, of course! I looked like some creepy-ass stalker. I'd look the other way too if I were you! I took deep breaths and tried to think of a plan.... I know! I'll wait for you after the game ends and things will just flow naturally between us. Right? I mean, we *are* sisters!

Just as I'd begun to feel more relaxed in such a strange environment, I must've missed something major. The entire arena was on its feet screaming "Kill him! Kill him! Kill him!" as players from opposing teams tore into each other! I mean, they were really going at it! Beer was spilling on all of us, and the anger on the faces of these fans literally scared the hell outta me. I watched you as you screamed and chanted with the masses, and in an instant, I felt so disconnected from you. You would never say something like that! Kill him? Seems a bit extreme, barbaric, and violent. Just not the you I thought I knew. Celebrating violence? Is that even a thing?

Things were just way too weird for me at that point, and I left. But I left confident in the fact that it wasn't you. Couldn't have been.

No way it was.

Absolutely not.

Or was it?

I mean, maybe one of your friends could have

leaned over and at least whispered something like, "First hockey game, huh? Oh, this is completely normal. Don't worry."

Just thinking out loud, but I'm not sure.

Super confused,

Your Sista

Pause, Reflect, & Discuss

- What traditions do you and your family practice that would be considered violent, dangerous, or extreme by other cultures? Why do you find this to be normal? How might these traditions alienate women of color and impede the deepening of these bonds with your sistas?

- What aspects of other cultures have you judged as extreme? (Examples: food, activities, music, language, religion, relationships, etc.)

14
Wait Your Turn!

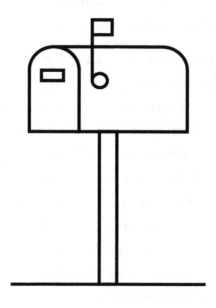

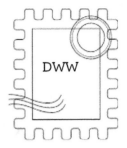

Dear White Woman,

Hey, sis. I asked myself this morning why I keep searching if it causes me so much pain. The truth is, I do it because I don't see many of my sistas doing it. And if you and I are ever to truly be allies, co-conspirators, and sisters, I have to keep searching for you. I can't give up. As soon as I give up hope, just like in a video game, we are returned to the starting line where our positions have been predetermined.

What you don't know is that I've been living in Texas for the last few years, but I think I'll move back to New England at the end of the year. Two years is good enough. The weather is beautiful here and the flowers are always blooming, but there seems to be a lot of mistaken identity that puts me back at square one in my search for you. I guess I should have known that no sister of mine would be caught down here with the current political climate being so polarized, fueled by the 2016 presidential election.

Anyways, just in case you might be passing through, I decided to head to the bakery that everyone here raves about. I knew that with your expertise in all things pastry chef (you remember how you used to help Mom with all the baking, right?), you might find your way to the Nothing But Cookies bakery. I actually hope Win one day asks me to marry her, and we serve these mini cookies at our wedding if they stand the test of time. (More about Win in another letter on another day. I promise!)

Nevertheless, I showed up with my sunglasses shoved back into my big hair and with an appetite large enough to hold all the baked cookies in the world. There seemed to be a bit of a line at the counter, but I was willing to wait for the joy that all the locals had spoken so highly of. As the line moved closer and closer to the counter, I noticed a woman stood next to the line as if she had formed her own line. She stared at all of us in the "official line" with a look of emptiness and superiority. You could just feel it, sis. Just as she turned away from us, it happened! She put her hair behind her ear in that twisty way you used to! 'Twas no stranger in that line; it was you!

Half stunned and half blown away, I swallowed hard and tried not to be too noticeably excited. I waited my turn at the counter and decided I would speak with you after the golden cookies were securely placed in my hands. With a cheerful and deeply southern accent, there came a "May I help whoever's next?" Well, as I moved forward, you stepped right up and began placing your order. You were pleasant, you were cheerful, and you were polite, but you were not "next." That day, you barely even looked at me, as you wrongfully took my turn in line. What blew me away was that the cashier saw what happened and said nothing! Nothing, sis! What is it about you white women sticking together? Is she on the payroll?

This could not have been you. After all, Ma always said we had home-training*, and we certainly were raised to wait our turn in line. Don't you remember? Or had you changed that much?

I waited for my second turn in line, got my goodies, and walked away. I simply did not have the energy. I thought about calling you on your behavior because if you had just said, "Excuse me; I'm late for my kid's birthday party. Do you all mind if I go next?" I would have understood and let you go ahead of me. But you didn't do that, and I just couldn't give you that time or energy today, white woman. I had so many things I wanted to say to you, but why waste my breath on someone who simply could not have been you?

I chose to enjoy my cookies and the rest of my day instead. While it had been another day without having found you, there would not be a dark cloud over it for me. I decided it would be a great day despite the fiasco at the bakery counter. I took my power back, just like Ma taught us as kids.

The real you would remember that too.

With love,
Your Sista

*Home-training – No, this does not refer to dogs or other animals. It is a set of manners, rules, and behaviors, spoken and unspoken, that children raised in traditional and stereotypical African American/Black homes have. Examples include but are not limited to: never addressing an adult by their first name, always responding "Yes?" when your name is called (not "What?"), never going in someone else's refrigerator without permission, saying "excuse me" when needing to interrupt an adult conversation (and that is only for real emergencies), and so many more. So yes, your children who do not follow these rules may be seen by some (remember, I do not speak for all) African American/Black families as rude or lacking "home-training." And, please, stop sharing drinks!

Pause, Reflect, & Discuss

- When was a time that you went against a standard way of being in society? (Examples: cut in a line, quoted a different price for an item at the store without a tag, had a conversation while being unaware of your volume or tone.)

- How might you have stepped in as an ally to help the situation at the counter? How might the trust that women of color have in you diminish due to your lack of action?

15
Happy Father's Day

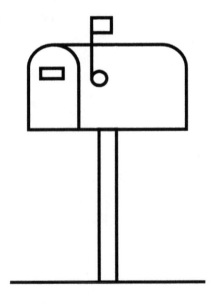

Dear White Woman,

Hey, sis. So I'm finally ready to talk about Dad's passing with you. But, before I share that pain here, I need to clarify one thing and teach you another. This is pretty heavy, so I won't be out searching for you today. Self-care today looks like sipping warm tea (ginger turmeric, not chai) and sharing a painful chapter of what you've missed.

Clarification. The Dad who passed away was not my biological father. He technically was my stepdad. As I sit here at my window surrounded by greenery, squirrels, and flowers, my "Daddy" is alive and well. That's how we knew him. We spent some weekends and school vacations with him and his side of the family in elementary school, and then he was in and out of our lives for various reasons, including substance abuse, until we became grown adults and made the decision to connect with him again. So generally, when I refer to "Dad" in any of my letters to you, I am talking about the one who raised me, provided for me, punished* me, encouraged me, tutored me, took me to piano and dance lessons, and cared for me.

Dad was a great provider. That was his way of showing love. He was a saver. He saved as many pennies as he could. Then at Christmas time he'd cash them in and give us each $500. We were required to give $100 of it to children in need, and that was never easy, but it taught us how to care for those who are less fortunate. Dad was many amazing things to us, but he had dark clouds that followed him. The dark clouds of addiction to alcohol and cigarettes made life challenging for him and challenging for us. I used to think to myself that he must've been miserable at home with us if he had to drink himself into an oblivion. But now I realize addiction knows no circumstances, race, economic status, or religion. It is no respecter of persons, as the religious folks say. Dad was indeed addicted to alcohol and cigarettes, but he set himself free one day. Cold turkey.

He'd had a tough medical diagnosis that made him walk away from his addictions without looking back. For two years, he was sober. He was a very different person. The dark clouds were gone, and he was a new man. He was very introverted, so he wasn't much of a talker when he was sober, but I didn't care since he was healthy again.

Then, one day, it started again. And, this time, it did not stop. It took a toll on him. It took a toll on us all. The family had separated, and Dad was living alone for the most part. His mom had passed, and we had grown up and found our own homes.

When we visited him, he seemed slower, or like normal aging conditions were setting in, like arthritis. Then one day, it was different. My partner at the time and I had come home to Washington, DC, and stayed with him until we could find a place of our own. I was in the shower, and my partner yelled to me to get upstairs as quickly as I could. I panicked and jumped out of the shower and went upstairs to the kitchen to find Dad slumped over the table barely able to breathe. I begged him to let me call an ambulance, and he wouldn't. It's crazy to think that in the Black community, our respect for our parents might go contrary to what deep down we know is best for them.

He was making cornbread to take to our church to add to what others had prepared to feed the homeless, like he did one Saturday out of each month. He wouldn't let me call the ambulance and wouldn't let me take him to the hospital, but he did let me finish the cornbread and take it into the city.

When I returned, I begged him to go to the hospital again, as he sat gasping for air. He said he knew it was pneumonia or COPD and that he had a scheduled appointment on Monday with the doctor anyways. So I secretly called immediate family members and said they should come to the area, because I thought Dad was going to die.

Monday came, and he went to see his doctor at the hospital. He was admitted, and they began running tests. It wasn't COPD or pneumonia.

It was stage four cancer.

It was everywhere. It had spread to his brain and his bone marrow. There was nothing they could do. He was in so much pain that he cried. Dad cried, sis. I'd only seen him cry once before then, and it was when the family separated. Our dad was crying.

I was working at a new school in the area, and there was a woman who looked just like you who said, "Kim, if your dad is in ICU, then you should be there with him." I stayed in the hospital day and night with Dad, waiting for him to get better. Family and friends came by to pray with him and to encourage him. The doctors decided not to share how bad off he was with him. And we respected that.

One day, the nurse came in and said, "I don't know why you're staying here with your dad. He's fine. He could live for months and months like this. Go home and shower and get some rest." So I did. I went home, I showered, and I rested. And, then I got the call. I was on my way back to the hospital when Mom called and said Dad had passed. The last words I heard him speak were "Obama. Obama. Obama." He died the day after history had been made.

From that Monday to the end were only eight days. We had eight days to say goodbye to Dad.

Now, I know you are not the best at expressing that you care, so I will guide you here. Care looks like using your words verbally or in a card to say, "I'm sorry for the pain you feel." Care looks like baking something and bringing it by. Care looks like asking me what I need to make it through this tough time. Care looks like helping to lift the burden of grief in any way you can. That's what care looks like. It's not enough to say you care. There must be action.

With care,

Your Sista

Punished – I believe you might call this grounded. The act of restricting access to pleasures, devices, free time, friends, etc.

Pause, Reflect, & Discuss

- What emotions came up for you reading this letter?

- What did you learn about care that came as a surprise to you? When have you struggled to *express* care to your sistas of color?

- How does your approach to grief clash with that of your sistas?

- Where do you see your own experiences of grief reflected in this letter?

16
All Money is Green

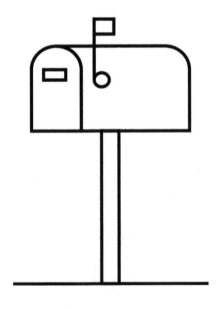

Dear White Woman,

I have a few extra minutes while I wait on one of my newest clients who is running late. I decided to make her appointment in the evening just in case we ran over in our time together. She was super excited to find a certified health and life coach of color. It is difficult to imagine that in such a major city women of color would have a hard time finding physical, mental, and emotional support from providers who look like them, understand them, and can relate to their lived experiences, but it is true. I'm excited to support her in her journey yet doubting my own journey of searching for answers in locating you and finding out who did this to you.

I guess I'm doubting because I'm thinking about my trip to the bank this morning. I left the bank feeling discouraged after trying to connect with someone who at the end of our meeting probably thought I needed a coach my damn self. I went in early to meet with the branch manager at the credit union where I've been a member for years to look at mortgage options for Win and me. That's right, sis! We're looking into buying our first home! While she hasn't popped the question yet, can't start planning for our future too soon, right? Maybe I'll be the one to pop the question first! Who knows, lol? So anyways, I arrived a few minutes before our scheduled appointment to make sure I didn't reinforce any stereotypes about folks of color showing up late everywhere they go. I sat in the small waiting area, listening for my name to be called. And then, it happened!

You emerged from your corner office facing the wooded area behind the plaza then looked around and yelled, "Kimberlee?" Well, I was the only one in the waiting area, but you seemed to be looking beyond me, as if you already knew I wasn't the Kimberlee you were looking for. I looked around with you to see if maybe someone else had my name. No one responded to your call, so I said, "Good morning," and extended my right hand with an "I'm Kimberlee." You shifted your papers and clipboard in your hands as if to say your hands were too full to shake mine and muttered, "Follow me."

We went into your office, and your decorations confirmed what I already knew. It was you! All of your decorations were yellow and purple just like you loved growing up. My favorite color was yellow, and yours was purple, so we always combined the two when we decorated our rooms. Purple is Win's favorite color too! I can't wait for you to meet her.

Anyways, the excitement was already stirring in my soul and was about to overflow when you smiled at me and began speaking about mortgage options. Even though you were smiling, something about your tone was off. Like you didn't recognize me or something. So I said, "You can call me Kimmy or Kimbo like all my family used to." You gave a courtesy laugh and kept it moving*. You finished up your speech by telling me how you would give me six months to fix up my credit report and to find a co-signer to help me qualify for this mortgage. And, just like that, I knew it wasn't you. How did you know what my credit looked like? What salary I was earning? That maybe I was buying this home by myself? You would never have made assumptions about my credit- worthiness without a conversation or pulling my credit. You never even asked what my budget was or if I'd taken my First-Time Homebuyers class. Maybe this is a rehearsed speech you give to anyone looking to buy a home, but knowing the historical barriers constructed for Black people in the real estate market would have lead you to begin your speech with something like, "We share this advice with all future homebuyers...."

Ugh! How could you say that to me? Did you know that I'd gone to college and graduated twice? *With a bachelor's degree and a master's degree?* Did you know I spoke three languages fluently? Did you know my credit took years to build and was as immaculate as that of the "Kimberlee" you'd imagined would show up today? Did you know that in my heart, I only came to this appointment because I was convinced to listen to the mortgage options instead of using our savings to pay for a house in cash?

You couldn't have known because you would've treated me very differently. I mean, I'm your sista! How could you not know?

My humanity and dignity once again discarded.

Tossed aside like it meant nothing.

Mmmm. No time to process right now.

Gotta go. My client is walking in.

Will write soon,

Your Sista

Kept it moving – Continued what you were saying or doing without pause for what I said.

Pause, Reflect, & Discuss

- What snap judgments have you made by looking at someone? (Examples: Asked a question to someone shopping in a store, assuming they were an employee; asking to speak to someone's manager, assuming it couldn't be them.)

- When was the last time you struggled to find a professional (doctor, nurse, specialist, counselor, yoga instructor, etc.) that looked like you? What did you do about it?

- Are you aware of the systemic lending bias and barriers to Black and brown people? Barriers holding back your Black and brown sisters who would like a home to call their own just like you would?

17
Who Asked You?

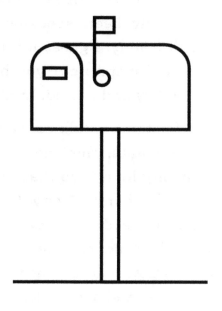

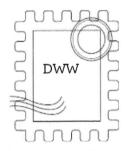

Dear White Woman,

I just pulled up at Blueberry Academy--you know, the boarding school in Connecticut. I will be here giving a few anti-racism talks during their diversity conference. Not too bad a ride, and I'm hoping to cast my net wider and to see if you might be here too. All of the faculty and staff have been gracious hosts and my bags have been taken to the guest house. I'm nervous for these talks since I've only been speaking on these topics with adults lately. I guess it'll be good to reconnect with and inspire our youth to take a stand against bigotry and hatred, huh?

In preparation for the pre-talk conversation I'm having with the adults, they have set me up nicely in the faculty lounge so that I can gather my thoughts beforehand. Everyone seems a bit hurried and stressed, and I've heard a few whispers of grades and comments being due in a few days, so that makes sense. There I am going over my notes and slides, deep in my own thoughts, when you walk into the lounge with another teacher! Could you have known that I was coming to Blueberry this weekend? No way! I don't recognize the other teacher, but I do recognize you after all these years! What do I say? What do I do? I don't want to interrupt because it seems that either he is new to Blueberry, or the copy machine is new, because you are explaining things very loudly and slowly to him.

I try really hard to mind my business, but you're my sister! Hurry up with this instructional lesson on how to use the copier already! I just have to have to *have to* speak with you before I address the faculty and staff! You are just as I remember you--you haven't let this guy get a word in edgewise, lol. Still the same sister I always knew.

I sit back smiling, watching you in action. You're still speaking pretty loudly and slowly, so I lean in to hear what you are teaching the newbie now. I hear, "If you need help writing your comments to send home to parents, you should visit the ESL [English as a second language] department." I watch the man's face change completely from bewilderment to complete and utter disgust.

His look says it all, sis. His eyes begged you to stop talking for one minute to let him speak, and you never did. You assumed he struggled with writing, reading, speaking, and comprehending English because he was Chinese. The horrific and embarrassing part of this instance is that when he finally got a chance to speak, he spoke English perfectly. He spoke with what is often referred to as an "American accent," whatever that means. He spoke it better than you. And who asked you to help him with the copier, his comments, or his English? Nobody! Another day, another unsolicited "helpful" white woman lending a hand.

All of a sudden, I just wasn't so sure it was you. I was so embarrassed. No sister of mine would make assumptions like that. After all, we come from a multi-cultural family, and we all speak English just fine. Couldn't you have just asked him if he needed any support given that he was new to the Blueberry community?

I don't know. It can't be you. Not here. Not like this.

I've gotta get my notes together, although I'd

rather ball up and cry watching this conversation happen in front of me. And now I have to go in and speak to strangers about anti-racism? If my own sister could say something so racist, how can I get up and give this talk?

So glad it wasn't you, 'cause I wouldn't want you to have become okay with that kind of nonsense.

Maybe I'll look for you at the next speaking engagement,

Your Sista

Pause, Reflect, & Discuss

- How do you decide who is and isn't American?

- Where are your ancestors from? How did they get to this country?

- How do your assumptions harm your sisters of color and destroy your bonds with them?

18
The Back of
the Bus

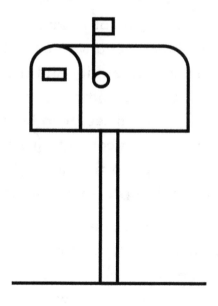

Dear White Woman,

You would be disappointed to know I took a break from the world of education, knowing that we are a family of educators, to work at a non-profit in the heart of downtown Boston for a bit. What a wild and crazy adventure it has been! First of all, you know I don't like being in crowds or riding no public transportation, girl! But I decided to see how the other part of the world lives, so I took the job. You have got to know this means I ride trains and busses and walk a lot! I meet with clients out in the community and then push the paperwork back in the office. Thankfully, they have a diversity committee I can be a part of in addition to my private consulting and coaching work, and that helps to fill the void of working more directly on things I feel passionately about.

So anyways, the other day on the train, I got on and sat near the exit so I could breathe and minimize my anxiety each time the doors opened. You know, I don't think you were around when we found out why I hate public transportation so much. Don't worry, I'll share that with you in another letter. I promise.

Anyways, I sat in a row that seemed to be unofficially reserved for young white men, but I didn't care. I pulled my book out and drowned myself in the world of fiction to take my mind off of the fact that I was enclosed in a dirty, packed train full of angry-looking people and their negative energy. Just as we pulled into the stop that is just a few stops from my home, a white woman a little younger than me gets on. I notice her curves and her style of dress and wonder if it could be you. I try not to stare but only two people on the earth wear earrings like that—you and me! You had suitcases and bags as if you'd made a special trip to town just to find me! You literally were looking for me too, sis!

Just as I decided to jump up and call your name, you came over to me! Can you believe it? You came to speak to me! I didn't have to say anything! But something wasn't right. You looked cold, and it was the middle of the summer. You looked empty. You stood in front of me, looked me in the eyes, and said, "I'm going to need your seat!"

My heart sank as I stood up and gave you my seat. You might even ask why I gave up my seat. But, sis, have you seen the news lately? White people have become unhinged. Random white people killing people in just about every public place possible. It's scary! I didn't know if she would kill me over a seat on a train! Then I'd be the latest news headline. So I gave it to her!

Anyways, it was clear it wasn't you. Ma taught us never to address anyone like that. So it could not have been you. But, even if it was, you certainly would have asked one of those strong white men, instead of me, to give up their seat for you. I was the only woman in the row and the only person of color, and somehow you chose me to surrender a seat for you. That's when I knew it wasn't you. You would have stood before expecting me to. Because you were never taught entitlement in our home.

As I recall, the story of Rosa Parks was drilled into us before we ever went off to anybody's elementary school, and you know what that means to our people. I mean, this lady might as well have said, "Get your ass to the back of the bus!" Rosa Parks was a strong young woman of character and strength with the intellect and precision to masterfully plan the particular bus route, bus, and time to intentionally take a seat. That's who she was, and I am one of her many sistas. So, no, it definitely wasn't you. Couldn't have been.

Just remembering this moment makes me sick to my stomach.

This was not you.

You are better than that,

Your Sista

Pause, Reflect, & Discuss

- Remembering that these letters are true stories, what part made you say to yourself, "Oh my, I would never do that!"?

- As bystanders watching this happen, why is it that none of the white people on the train intervened? How did the lack of intervention shape the author's views about being able to count on white people as allies or co-conspirators?

19
May I Help You Find Something?

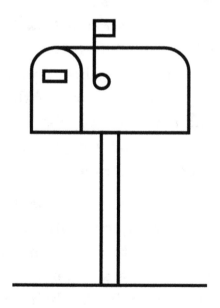

Dear White Woman,

While I am happy to report that I will soon be leaving the world of trains and busses to return to commuting in the car, I am also feeling like it's time to turn the corner in my love life. Sis! I'm making so many changes! I guess you know what they say: "The only constant in life is change," or something like that, lol. Anyways, I visited the jewelry store yesterday because I believe it's time to ask Win if she will marry me. Now, I know you'll have trouble believing I'm gay because of how we were raised in the evangelical church. But sis! I am so happy! I've been out of the closet for years now and am much happier being my true self! So folks that don't accept that layer of my identity no longer bother me.

Anyways, I looked at so many rings that my mind was 'bout ready to explode with all the choices and options in that store. The employees were too busy talking to one another to even notice I might have needed help. As their conversation about everything and nothing rolled on and on, I noticed an overwhelming accent that seemed like a combination of Washington, DC, and North Carolina. It sounded like me, lol! Or, *like you!*

I looked up, and there you were with the keychain for the display cases around your wrist and your arms folded with your hand to your chin just like you always did. Remember how Ma used to knock your hand down and say, "Your neck is strong enough to support your head!"? Oh, those were the days, lol. Anyways, you looked up, so I turned away thinking you caught me staring at you or something. You were moving in my direction, looking right at me, as if you recognized me too. Weird, right? My heart started pounding through my chest, and I didn't know what to say.

You walked right past me to the customer who had just entered and asked him how he was doing and if you could help him find anything. It was like the music stopped. My heart slowed to an ache, and I began falling into the invisible—yet familiar—place of shame, confusion, longing, and anger. I could not help but notice not only did you greet this man, but so did your two coworkers over at the other end of the counter. Suddenly, your conversation no longer mattered, and all of you cared more about helping this potential customer than you did about finishing your chat. This is the same conversation that was too important to stop when I walked in or when I was visibly in need of assistance.

Now, Daddy was absent for most of our lives, but Ma sure ain't raise us like that. Especially not to be that way toward members of our own family or tribe. I could not help but think that you and your coworkers somehow believed this man was more valuable than I was. That he was going to spend money you assumed I did not have, so I wasn't worth your time. I'd love to pretend that this implicit bias I spend so much time teaching about in workshops was based on the fact that he was a man. However, we know it was because he was white, because, after all, Black women are just the bottom of the barrel within this social hierarchy. Why else would you and your coworkers greet this man, yet not even acknowledge my presence? I'll wait for your answer....

Listen, it's not like we are looking for perfection from you because perfection ain't real. All I wanted was a "Let me know if I can help you find something." Or maybe the other associates could have reminded you to help me first, given that I entered before the white man.

While that accent really had me believing it was you, I knew deep down it couldn't have been. You were the type of person who would notice this exact same thing happening to someone else and stand up for them no matter who it was. This was something Ma and so many of our mentors instilled in us.

The ring set I was looking to finance cost $25,000, but after the treatment I received, I decided not to give my business to your store and wondered if maybe it was the universe saying it wasn't time to pop the question. I don't know.

And the man? Oh, he was "just window shopping."

Angry and sad,

Your Sista

Pause, Reflect, & Discuss

- What about the author signaled to the employees that she was not worthy of their attention?

- How many times have you witnessed this? If the answer is never, and this is happening every day and everywhere, why have you never noticed it?

- Where will the author go to purchase jewelry in the future? How might her network, knowing about her experience, impact business at that store?

20
Got a Tissue?

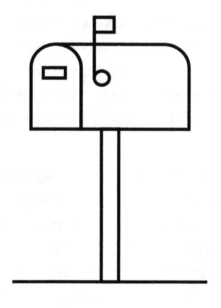

Dear White Woman,

As promised, I need to talk to you about why I hate using public transportation. You know I'm one of those who are all about saving the planet, and I always have been, but I cannot do public transportation, sis. We found out a few years ago that I'm an empath, or what is sometimes called a highly sensitive person. I literally sat in busses and trains soaking up other people's energy--good and bad--like a sponge. A counselor framed it perfectly for me when she said, "Kim, all it means is that you experience really high highs and really low lows, and that there is no barrier between the energy that is yours and that of others."

Some people call it a gift and say things like, "I wish I could feel and show empathy," or "If only I could be an empath." For me, it sometimes feels like being tortured. I sometimes wake up at night with dreams of things that are announced on the news the next day or go into deep bouts of depression about a war happening in another country. Don't even mention natural disasters. Ugh! I even sometimes feel the illnesses of family members and friends before they happen. It's a gift and a curse all at the same time. Who else do you know that spends a week crying over a whale that washes up on the beach that can't be saved?

Right, nobody.

Thankfully, I have a counselor who helps me to set boundaries with such an outward-facing life and to work through the lows. Now, the highs? They are truly a gift.

An empath through and through,

Your Sista

Pause, Reflect, & Discuss

- Are you or do you know of someone who is an empath? Describe them.

- How did reading this letter impact you? What messaging have you gotten about expressing feelings as a woman? Are white women and women of color perceived differently when it comes to expressing emotions?

- How might the empath in the author impact her search for you?

- If you are an empath, how do you balance the energy that comes from the ills of racism with that of social justice movements? If you are not an empath, how might a lack of empathy work against your goals when exploring racist ideology and behaviors?

- Can you name a "gift" you possess that few know about or that may be seen as rare?

21
You Always *Did* Ruin a Good Movie!

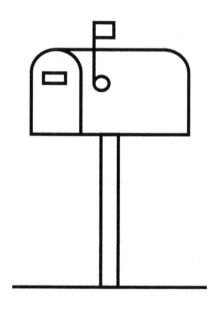

Dear White Woman,

Well, I must say that I am renewed in my energy and feeling quite optimistic about finding you. I went to hear a motivational speaker, and her presentation convinced me that I could do absolutely anything! So I took a few days to relax and rejuvenate, and then I set out again to find you.

As a part of my relaxation, I decided to go to the movies to see what I thought would be a really good thriller. Do you remember how we would stay up late watching scary movies together? Mom definitely could not find out, because those things were certainly of the devil! Anyways, the movie was playing late at night, but I didn't care. I just wanted to feel the thrill of a scary movie for an hour and a half.

Well, don't you know that up the stairs comes a group of young women giggling to themselves. I wasn't sure what was so funny, but I heard a giggle that sounded all too familiar. Growing up with you, there were many things that we were known for as sisters, but our laughs were always at the top of the list. People used to say, "Chile*, I know that laugh from a mile away," and they still do. So I sat up in my fancy recliner seat and cranked my neck in the darkness to see if I could spot you in the group.

Closer and closer as you reached the top of the stairs and started down my row, I became more and more sure of the sound of your laugh. I just knew it was you! You came closer, and I thought I would end my search that very night because you had come to visit me in my row at a movie theater! As you approached your assigned seat, you realized that it was right next to mine. You stopped dead in your tracks after taking one look at me. You motioned for one of your friends to sit next to me, and they laughed and declined the invitation as well. None of you wanted to sit next to me, as if I smelled awful. Can you imagine how much that hurt? The movie started playing and your laughter ended, as one of your friends sank down into the chair pissed that she had to sit next to me. I spent the whole movie just trying to hold it together, to calm the pit in my stomach and the ache in my heart.

Is Blackness contagious, dirty, smelly, disgusting, or scary?

Maybe it is none of these things.

Or, maybe it is all of these things.

Why else would my own sister refuse to sit next to me?

But, that's just it.

She wouldn't.

So I knew it couldn't have been you. But none of your friends thought to say to you, "What's your problem? Sit down! The movie is going to start!" Like, none of them?! Where was the you I just know would've sat beside me and whispered, "I'm so sorry. They are not the women I thought they were, and I'm going to let them know that as soon as we leave this theater."

The movie sucked. Or was it my interaction that ruined "movie night" for me?

I am hurting and screaming inside.

Starting to question why my love for you has been unconditional,

Your Sista

*<u>Chile</u> — Not a pepper used to make spicy food! It's the way the word child is often pronounced when someone is trying to make a point. It rhymes with while. Examples could be, but are not limited to, "Chile, you don't know what you have 'til you lost it," or "Chile, you betta come on in here and get some of these greens!", or "Chile you better take that broke-down thing back to the store and get yo' money back." You get the point, right?

Pause, Reflect, & Discuss

- Why was it that the group of young women felt uncomfortable sitting next to the author? ("They didn't know her," is an unacceptable answer. Every time you attend a movie that is sold out, you or someone from your group ends up next to someone you don't know.)

- What decision do you think the author and her friends made going forward about trips to the movies because of this interaction with the group of young white ladies?

- Can you find someone to role-play the post-theater conversation promised by the committed ally and her group of friends?

22
What Would It Take for You to See Me?!

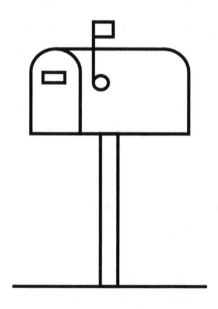

Dear White Woman,

Well sis, I hit a huge bump in the road. Just when I was making so much progress in my search for you, I took a major blow. I am now living life as a person with a physical disability. I know, you're wondering how this happened to me. Well, remember those dance classes you quit so long ago? I never quit; instead, it became a passion for me. I have spent three decades of my life, at least two hours a day—every day—practicing dance, coaching dance, choreographing pieces, or performing.

The doctors say this is what led to my injury. One day I was fine, and the next day, I woke up, put my feet on the floor, and then collapsed. My left foot and ankle had gone into complete tendon failure, sis. I could not walk, run, jump, leap, climb stairs, go to the bathroom, shower, walk my dog, or do anything for myself. I was in for the toughest ride of my life, as I had to have complete and total reconstruction of my foot and ankle. Reading the post-surgical report made me nauseous, seeing that they had literally cut my foot and ankle into pieces and then put them back together with screws and staples. Who even knew staples came that large?

Anyways, I am barely mobile at all and living all of my active time on one leg and traveling on a scooter. The doctor doesn't know how long it will be before I am able to walk on my own again, so I have been trapped in the house since my last letter to you. I'm barely able to do anything on my own; I need help bathing, cooking, and getting dressed too. Ma has been here helping me, and yesterday, she was truly a godsend.

I was suffering from cabin fever and needed to get out of the house. You know how stubborn I can be sometimes, sis. I didn't believe Ma when she said that the amount of work it would take to get me out of the house would just tire me out and put me in a bad mood. I insisted and persisted, and off we went to the mall. I was so happy to be in the car and out around other people that I nearly forgot about my lack of mobility. Ma parked the car and pulled the scooter out of the trunk. She pulled it around to the side so that I could travel through the parking lot on the scooter instead of her dropping me off at the door. I was soooo humble, lol.

We got into the store and of course Ma got taken by the beautiful linens right there at the door! She wanted to stop and look through that section, so I kept scooting right along until...well, until, just like Ma said, I got tired. So I stopped for a moment to catch my breath. I rested one hand on a rack and the other on my scooter for balance while waiting for Ma to finish in the linens section. I kept her in my line of sight in case I needed to yell to her for help. And just then, I heard a familiar accent.

It had to be from the DMV (DC, Maryland, and Virginia, not the driver's license place)! I looked for Ma in excitement to let her know that I swore I heard your voice. Ma had been calling you the prodigal daughter (biblical reference of course) for as long as I can remember, and I think she may have given up hope. But here was hope standing right next to my scooter! I motioned for Mom to come over, and she put up her finger to ask for a moment. The more you talked to the sales associate, the more I listened. The more I listened, the more I was certain that it was your voice. The accent and tone were definitely you. While I did not recognize you physically, that didn't stop me because no one else had a voice like yours. Even when you laughed, like I said before, I knew it was you!

Then you turned around, looked into my eyes-- that were filled with fatigue from getting around on one leg--and asked, "Can I help you with something?" I wondered why you thought I needed help. I rested my hand on a rack nearby to steady myself again and saw the price tag on the merchandise hanging on this particular rack. Then, I noticed that you and the sales associate moved your conversation much closer to me— like, right next to me, actually. You paused and asked me again if I needed help. Damnit! Here we go again. Not even the disabled are exempt if they are brown or Black. You literally accused me of plotting to steal this jacket. I was pissed at this point. How could my sister believe that I, someone clearly struggling to move at all, would steal a jacket? Where was I going to put this jacket? In my scooter's basket?

I called for mom and asked her to hurry. I told her what happened, and right then and there she confirmed my fears with her response, "Well, you know how they are, Kim." That let me know she indeed had given up hope of ever finding you. She had resigned herself to the fact that you were never coming home. She bought into the stereotypes about women like you, white women. That's what she meant by the "they" in "Well, you know how they are, Kim." She meant that she could count on you to be suspicious of brown and Black people; predict you'd think we don't belong in "expensive" establishments; assume you'd think they are up to no good, and the list goes on. Unfortunately, Ma is no different than the countless number of Black and brown women who actually had hope of a sisterhood at some point and have simply given up after experiencing one too many microaggressions.

How could I blame her? Without saying it directly, you accused me of wanting to steal a jacket!

I know I was mistaken in believing it was you, but Ma taught us to see the humanity in everyone.

You would have seen me as your sister first, and not ever thought I was there to steal from your store. When you asked if you could help me, you would have *meant* it. You would have offered me a seat where I could rest and let me know that if there was anything I was interested in seeing or trying on that you would help me.

But you didn't.

You didn't see me.

My humanity.

Remember the lyrics to the song "Give Me Your Eyes" by Brandon Heath that Ma taught us? "Give me your eyes for just one second. Give me your eyes so I can see everything that I keep missing. Give me your love for humanity. Give me your arms for the broken-hearted, the ones that are far beyond my reach. Give me your heart for the ones forgotten. Give me your eyes, so I can see."

Don't you remember?

I will never forget. And for that reason, I will never give up.

Why don't you see my humanity? Or why aren't

you trying to see my humanity as hard as I'm trying to see yours?

Your Sista

Pause, Reflect, & Discuss

- Have you ever been followed around a store? If so, what did that feel like? Have you ever watched it happen to someone else? Did you intervene?

- Have you ever been falsely accused of something? What did that feel like?

- How might words like "suspicious, uncommon, loitering" be words that can be translated to mean Black or brown people? These are the words being used in customer service training for employees being trained to protect the inventory that's on the sales floor.

23
Living on Borrowed Strength

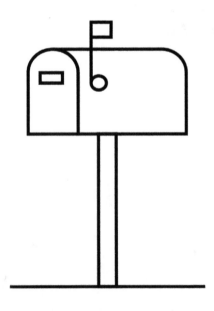

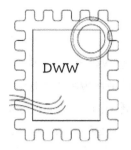

DWW

Dear White Woman,

I'm sitting here writing to you about the silent and sworn commitment to the ideal of strength. We, as Black women, have passed down this idea of strength from generation to generation. We are so proud to make sure we come last on our list of priorities that we make sure no one ever sees us sweat because we always have it together. (Whatever the "it" is.) We are the first to arrive to work to show how dedicated we are, we never take days off, and we are the last to leave. All of this while we work really hard to make sure we go unnoticed and keep all of the people around us happy and comfortable. Especially white people, sis. We change our style of dress, our voices, our hair, our cars, our homes, our cooking, our reading selections—all to keep white folks comfortable. Why do we do this? Why do we keep suffering in the name of this mythological strength? Then we get so confused by all the random illnesses we have. It angers me that I'm in my 40s and still feel guilty when I take one of my vacation days off. Why the hell do I do that? Then we get to the end of the year and have a pile of use 'em or lose 'em days that we wave goodbye to. And for what? What prize do we win? *To die early? To live in vain?*

I guess deep down, death has me thinking about this today. Our aunt died last week, sis. She was in her early 60s, and she's gone. I think about the rounds of cancer she battled, and how much energy I've given to keeping folks comfortable instead of living and being me to the absolute fucking fullest. Like that F-bomb, a few years ago, I wouldn't have put it in this letter for fear that it would make you uncomfortable. But no more of that. Life is too short, and now losing our aunt at a time when I was told I needed to have a growth removed from my mouth has simply pissed me off. It has reminded me, as I wait to find out if it was cancerous or not, that life is precious, and I was put here to be myself fully. To show up for myself fully. To embody who I am and the dreams that fill my heart and imagination every single god-damned day. Isn't this what we're all here for?

I sat down to write to you about our aunt on our biological dad's side passing away, but I guess I'm writing to remind myself to be more like you, since that's what we gotta do to get anywhere in this white world. I once heard a white man on a reality television show say to his daughter, "Here is Point A, and there is Point B. Do whatever you have to do, to whomever you have to, to reach your destination." I remember being so offended at the thought of stepping on other people to get ahead, of doing whatever I had to do to my own sister for me to reach one of my own goals.

But at 40-something, I am beginning to understand it more.

It leaves me with one question, though. If we both put ourselves first, how can we make room for each other?

Wondering if I should lower my standards,

Your Sista

Pause, Reflect, & Discuss

- What did this letter leave you feeling? (Feeling, not thinking.)

- In what ways do you suppress parts of who you are? Deny dreams that you have? And if your answer is, "I don't," does being white have anything to do with that?

- How can you become a place of support (or safety) where women of color can show up authentically and fully?

24
Head of the Table

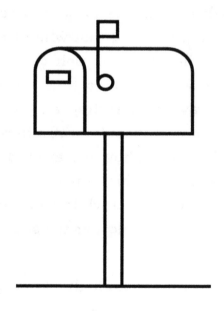

Dear White Woman,

Well, sis, I'm back at it. I'm looking for you. Where are you? I know you're wondering how my results turned out. I am cancer-free! Whew! What a relief!

Anyways, I have settled into a new leadership role quite nicely and am looking forward to effecting change in this organization. It is so exciting how nice and welcoming everyone has been to me since I began in this new role. Yet even as I write this, I'm noticing that when I put on my senior admin hat, I find myself code-switching. You know, where I have to tone my exuberant self all the way down and speak perfect King's English? Yeah, that. People have offered to take me to lunch and to show me around the town. I had a personal tour just a few days ago of the surrounding towns, and while I just loved it, it was exhausting not being able to speak my native tongue.

Why don't I sound too excited? I knew you would

read between the lines, sis. You always know just what to say and exactly how I feel. I was excited! Honestly! Until I met the member of the board who reminded me of you and our childhood. Although you always knew how to get things rolling in the right direction, I couldn't help but feel it was overbearing and too much at times. And sure enough, that's exactly what happened with this lady.

Just as I sat down at the head of the table and listened to welcomes and introductions, I noticed the curly hair of one of the members. She hadn't looked in my direction at all since the start of the meeting but seemed to hog airtime with quite a few "important announcements that were pertinent to the meeting's agenda." The rise and fall of her voice sounded just like yours! The way she tapped the end of her pencil in her other hand while she spoke was just like you! She tucked her hair behind her ear just like you, and I was sure it had to be you!

Just as she finally turned to face me as she was talking, she thanked everyone for introducing themselves and prompted me to introduce myself. I thought, *If I'm the head of this committee, why do I need an invitation to introduce myself?* But I shook it off and briefly thanked everyone for the warm welcomes and proceeded. After I shared a little about me and my story, she seemed uneasy. She was shifting back and forth in her seat, as I proceeded to move through the meeting's agenda. When I wrapped up, she finally raised her hand and asked if there was time for questions. I quickly reassured her that all questions would be answered, as there was time built into the agenda for this. As I looked around, nobody seemed to have a question except for her.

And just like missing a shot at the buzzer, her words plunged me into the pit of disappointment: "By introducing yourself, I meant that you would share your qualifications with the group."

Did she need me to prove why I was sitting at the head of the table instead of her?

Did she need me to name my degrees? My colleges? My certifications? My former places of employment?

Was she second-guessing what I chose to share? What I wanted people to know about me? I wonder if she even heard a word I said, or was she all up in her head waiting for me to stop so she could instruct me to do it the white way, I mean the right way.

Why did I have anything to prove to her?

That's just it.

I didn't.

So, I didn't.

I replied, "I have shared what I needed to share to give you some insight into my passions and into who I am, and a quick online search can fill in the rest." I mean, couldn't she just say that she was super interested in knowing where I grew up or where I'd gone to college? But what my qualifications were?! Ugh!

Of course, once again, it wasn't you, sis.

Annoyed but persisting,

Your Sista

Pause, Reflect, & Discuss

- When you are asked to share about yourself in a group setting, how does it serve you to list aspects of your resume? What satisfaction does it bring and to whom?

- What does this white woman's need to hear the author "credentialize" herself say about how she finds value in herself and in others? How does this need prevent her from connecting with women of color?

25
Meet Christopher!

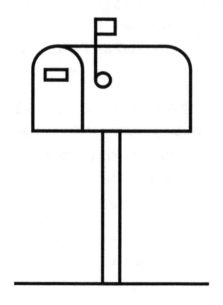

Dear White Woman,

It's my birthday today! And you know that every year for however long it was, we'd go to the zoo together on my birthday! Last year on my birthday, my own national holiday (!), a bunch of us went to a zoo where an exhibit had dinosaurs inspired by that new Jurassic Park movie! It was so much fun and scary too! Not sure what new exhibits they have this year, but I am so excited. Although I'm in my 40s, I will always be just as excited to go to the zoo as I was when I was five years old.

I already picked out my outfit, got my sunglasses and my fan 'cause you know I'm always sweating! But this year, I am wearing sneakers! The days of wearing heels everywhere I go are over for this girl!

I'm excited to see the new male lions 'cause you know a sista was depressed after Christopher, the lion at the zoo in Boston that I visited each year on my birthday, without fail, passed away. I see your left eyebrow raised like we used to do when we were confused, so yes, I'll explain. Two years ago, I showed up so excited to visit him and to see what he was up to. Sis, that whole empath thing had me! I felt so connected to that lion in so many ways that folks who are not empaths or animal lovers will never understand. But, sis, oh my God.

I got there, and they had put up a piece of printer paper announcing Christopher's death. *Literally, sis. A piece of cheap-ass copier paper.* I stood there crying in the middle of the zoo. My guy had moved on from here. Christopher was gone. Do you know he is my screen saver and wallpaper on my computer to this day? I miss him, and so our home is filled with pictures and statues of lions in nearly every room, and I feel him near me always.

On a lighter note, after fighting Boston's traffic to get there, we made it! The line was short, and my season pass got us in quick! And don't you know? The big deal this year is the lion exhibit because of the new male lions that replaced

Christopher. I went in and took a few pictures, and I was pleasantly surprised by the plaque they made in Christopher's honor. Thankfully, that plaque replaced the piece of copier paper.

Just as I started to walk away from the exhibit, a little white boy ran up to me and started roaring at me. I cracked up laughing with a smile from ear to ear! I bent down and started roaring right back at him! He smiled and laughed so loud! He kept right on roaring at me, and you know I had to indulge him because I love kids!

"Johnny! Johnny!" the woman headed in my direction called to him. I couldn't make out her face until she looked at me. She rushed to him and yanked him away in a flash. And as she scooped him up in her arms, she held him close and gave me the look that a momma bear would give any human who got anywhere near her cubs. I lowered my shades to see more clearly because I was certain I knew this woman. There was something about how much she cared for her son that reminded me of you and how we would volunteer at youth groups together in the community and at church. You loved the kids and would do anything to protect them from harm. *That's it!* That was the look you gave me! You thought I was going to harm him? You thought I was going to harm him! Instead of thanking me for entertaining your son, who had wandered off without you noticing, you gave me a look that said *Stay away from my son!*

And in that moment, without intending to, you taught your white son how to see Black and brown people.

Dangerous.

Scary.

Threatening.

I know you want to explain how you would have done that no matter who he was being entertained by, but given the historical implications of relationships between Black and white people, this was different. Why didn't you just remind Johnny of your rules about speaking to strangers and then thank me from the bottom of your goddamn heart for keeping an eye on him for you?

Anyways, I have to tell you that I had taken the

day off from searching for you so that I could honor and celebrate my own birthday. But watching you react to your own sister like that made me want to give up searching for you at all. So while the child-loving spark I saw in your eye reminded me of our childhood caring for our younger siblings and teaching them to be loving and compassionate towards a troubled world, I know deep down it wasn't you.

While finding you would've been a nice birthday present, my trip to the zoo will have to be enough. I am enough.

For today anyways.

I forgive you,

Your Sista

Pause, Reflect, & Discuss

- What lesson did the woman teach her son while interacting with the author?

- If you are a parent, what lessons have you unintentionally taught your children when it comes to interacting with people of color?

26
Do This Today!

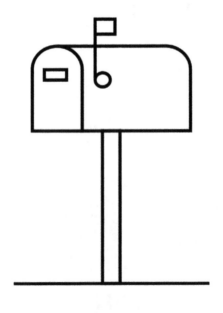

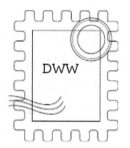

DWW

Dear White Woman,

I'm taking a break and caving to all the pressure I feel around me not to invite you to come back home. There is so much that I have to teach you before you can be seen with me in public. And even more so if you actually want to come home to stay. To heal. To reconnect. To live. To be in relationship for the first time with so many of your sisters. You've got to take my advice without questioning, nitpicking, or saying things like, "I'm so confused. Wait, I have a question." Just trust me on this. I'm one of the ones who wants to see you come home, and I know what you need to do to fit in around here and to invite your family members to trust you. So just listen and follow what I say, please.

P.S. It's not sugar-coated, 'cause we ain't got time to make it pretty for you.

Sis, first of all, stop staring at people you don't know. It makes you look rude and comes off like you question whether they are worthy of being in your presence or not. So stop that! And, stop it, today! Before we move on. Yes, I know you don't do it on purpose. But there is a reason, and I'll invite you to take some time to figure out that reason. Do you do it because you wonder why someone you didn't expect to be in your white space is there? Or maybe because the white glare/gaze has been passed down from generation to generation. You watched the white adults around you do it, and you learned to mimic it. They learned it from their adults who learned it from theirs. And so forth, and so on. It's like when I get really tickled and say, "Yes, indeed!" Mom does the same thing. And grandmother does it too!

Second, when people go deep (in conversations or interactions, I mean), stay in the water. Don't jump out with your grunt, your one-word response, or your silence. You may do that because you're uncomfortable, but it comes off as rude, or that you don't care about or want to be close to your sisters. And, please refuse to cry when someone calls you out on your silence. And, we're not talking about tears that mean you've been moved emotionally by the content of a conversation. No, I mean the tears that say you're embarrassed because someone has called you on your silence or grunts. Those tears become weapons to make sure that no one ever dares to call you on any of your perceived imperfections or flaws again. They disrupt, derail, and deter meaningful conversations and connections. Sis, squeeze every muscle in your body to stop those types of tears from flowing. And, if they still sneak out of the corners of your eyes, share out loud that they are a sign of your socialization and upbringing and they are yours to deal with. They are not the responsibility of anyone else. The show must and should go on.

Third, stop hogging the airtime. You know that rule we use with students? *"Three before me."* Use it! This normally happens during conversations that don't go very deep emotionally. In these instances, you come off as rude, or not self-aware. And the fact that you ramble on and only have so much to say about things that aren't even matters of the heart also makes you look like you need to demonstrate how much you know or have read in a book or how much better you are than others. It also makes you look like you don't care when you're either silent or offer up a meaningless grunt or single word, especially when it really counts. For me, it's not how much you know, it's how deep you can go, how much you can be present and connected in community. So be quiet and listen for a change. But, if the subject goes deep emotionally, lean in, and speak up. And don't pat yourself on the back for a two-word response, either.

Fourth, sis, this one really pisses some people of color off, 'cause we can see it from 100 miles away in the dark with no flashlight. The overly nice allies that are ready to prove how dedicated they are to social justice by pasting an ear-to-ear smile on their face and speaking in soprano the entire time? Yea, those. The problem with these folks is they are working so hard to prove themselves that they end up pushing us farther away by reminding us (in all of their niceness) that we don't belong. I met one of these at a Black Lives Matter event where the greeter at the door held my hand for at least five minutes while she welcomed me. Mind you, she held all the white folks' hands that showed up, um, oh, that's right, she didn't hold their hands at all. They got brief smiles, brief greetings, and a pat on the back. If that! Later, at the conclusion of the event, after the announcement had been made that EVERYONE could join the speaker downstairs for refreshments and a book signing, the same smiley white woman approached us in the sanctuary where we were chatting with our white woman friend to say, "You all are ALSO welcome to join us downstairs for refreshments and the book signing." Didn't she know that I understood English and knew that I was a part of EVERYONE? Sis, I hope you ain't one of those smiley overly "helpful" white women holding strangers' hands for way too long. Not a good look.

Fifth....Ugh, sis, I have to go. I have a client coming in at six who has made so many strides in these areas. This is why I believe in you! Because I see the progress in my clients. If they can do it, you can do it too. Don't worry. I'll write again with more tips for you.

Now, sis, given that all of this is new to you, I understand that the journey home may be unforgiving in its turbulence. I need you to understand why developing rock-solid resilience through the turbulence is so important for me. For us.

If you can't abandon the kidnapper's customs and find your way home to me, the very fabric of our family and thus our society is at stake.

Please don't abandon me,

Your Sista

Pause, Reflect, & Discuss

- Did any aspects of the author's advice make you want to give up?

- Which pieces of advice were simply unbelievable? Did you dismiss those with thoughts like, "She definitely isn't talking about me"? Or, "I don't do that. I would never do that"?

- Have you ever had to take direction from a Black or brown woman? What did it feel like?

27
More
American
Than You

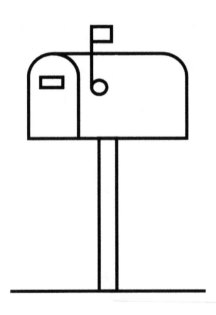

Dear White Woman,

Hey sis, I decided to be very alert going in to work today since you could literally be anywhere. But, honestly, I am reminded of a time where my guard was all the way down, and I just was not prepared for what was to come. I was working at Orange Country Day School near Boston, where I was the only Black adult on the faculty. Have you ever been the only person of your race on a work team of dozens? Hundreds? It's hard to describe the disorientation and distress it can cause if you've never experienced it firsthand. I had been working there for four years, and I had just discussed with my supervisor the idea of spending the rest of my career there, all the way to retirement.

Anyways, at the end of this particular day we had a faculty meeting, and one of the topics on the agenda was debriefing one of our recent speakers brought in to discuss diversity, equity, and inclusion. Many teachers and staff members weighed in to share their opinions and to ask questions. I listened and did not participate for the sole reason that I think they expected me to weigh in on all things diversity, you know? And I just didn't feel like it! Just then, a white male teacher spoke up to share his thoughts.

"Well, I'm so glad we're discussing this now," he stated, "because I tried to have this conversation years ago in my classroom. Now you've got to imagine that the Asian kids were sitting over here, and the Black kids were sitting over here, and the American kids were sitting over here." Now, sis, the entire world stopped spinning in that moment for me. *Literally stopped.* I had just talked to Ma days before about why we have to be called Black or African American instead of American. This was right after the Charleston church shooting. So here I was in a room where a white man had just said that I wasn't American.

But, sis, I was born here, my parents were born here, my grandparents were born here, my great-grandparents were born here, and my great-great-grandparents and those before them helped build this country after being kidnapped and enslaved centuries ago. Hell, I am as much a part of the American story as anyone will ever be. Meanwhile, this man's family had only been here in this country for a few generations. How is it that he was more "American" than I was? Clearly, he meant white kids when he said American kids.

Honestly, sis, I could have processed and dealt with what he said. It was ignorant, and he didn't know any better. I'm guessing he didn't even hear himself. He kept right on talking like he hadn't offended anyone. What wounded me most, and broke me, was the silence of my white sisters in the room. Many who look just like you, sound just like you, act just like you, remained silent. No sister of mine would have let this man say that we weren't American without checking him! Why didn't anyone speak up? What's that about? Did they not notice it? Did they notice it and not dare "rock the boat"?

This hurt me so deeply that I took off work for a few days and felt suddenly so alone. I wrote a letter to the school community and read it aloud while I sobbed in front of all those people—all those white people. I literally stood there vulnerable in front of all my colleagues reading and sobbing and sobbing and reading. I stayed in my apartment on campus all alone and barely came out. I filed a complaint with HR to discuss all of the many times when race was indeed a factor in the way that I was treated, but nobody could see it except me. A committee looked into it, and of course they found that there was "no racism" in my day-to-day interactions. It was all in my mind. Of course. And you already know the committee was made up of folks who all identified as white. Could you imagine an all-male committee telling a woman, "No honey, there was no sexism involved there. You're strong, you'll get through it, right?" People trapped so deep in their insulated identity blows my mind. They also scare the shit out of me.

So you know what, sis? I quit!

I quit working there. I quit hoping for some sort of familial bond. I quit searching for you among those women.

I left, and my job search landed me in Texas. And that time, when my guard came down, love found me.

I've gotta run. Will share more in the next letter.

Love you, sis,

Your Sista

Pause, Reflect, & Discuss

- Who does the title American belong to?

- What does American mean to you? Who are you leaving out of that narrative?

- Have you ever used the word American to mean white? Like, "America's favorite pie, or America's favorite pastime?"

- Have you ever been in an organization or group where you felt isolated, unseen, unappreciated, based on a layer of your identity? Did anyone have your back?

28
Love. Found.
Me.

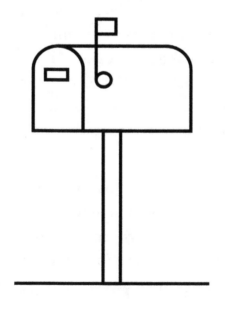

Dear White Woman,

So, as I said, my search took me from New England all the way to Texas. I was hell-bent on joining a community in San Francisco, but the stars aligned, and Texas was it.

One of the first things I did as a new hire in Texas was to attend the New Hire Dinner. I met what felt like a million people at this dinner and heard so many personal stories. I had a chance to be introduced to the other new hires, and then we ate dinner and shared stories, fears of being in a new city, and plans for the future. While I had met quite a few people, there was one in particular I hadn't said much to other than, "Hello, nice to meet you."

On the way out, I walked out with this person. She didn't say much, and she listened a lot. We got to the end of the block where our cars were parked and should have gone our separate ways, since the streetlights were already on, but we didn't.

We stood there underneath that streetlight for hours talking about everything and nothing all at the same time. There was an energy that drew us to one another, and we instantly became the best of friends. I'm pretty sure we spent every weekend in one way or another together. But we were just friends. Really good ones though, lol.

Having recently broken up with my ex-girlfriend at that time, I was suddenly free every afternoon and every weekend. And the two of us found a way to fill those days—and to fill them together. Movies, the mall, restaurants, arcades, bookstores, candle shops, candy stores, smoothie shops, hair salons, and so on! We were besties and didn't mind spending every free minute together.

I remember the first time someone asked me if I was in love with her. "Um, no!" That was my answer the first time and every time after that. People saw something between us that neither one of us could see. And that was the magic of it all. Our relationship was founded on a friendship that changed our worlds and formed a new one that belonged to the two of us, together. That friendship kept me grounded in so many ways, until she kissed me.

Then the heavens basically opened up and applauded what angels had been holding their breath hoping to see.

Suddenly, I could see her, and she could see me.

She became the love of my life.

And, just like that, love found me. And yes, if you're wondering, this is Win!

Was it always rainbows and sunshine? No. No love story ever is. But I knew she was my person because the tough times never made me want to run from her. For the first time in my life, I wanted to dig in, to learn, to grow in love, and to be the best me I could be. For her. For me. For us.

I am forever grateful because love found me, saw me, and rescued me.

I giggle and smile to myself, as I keep repeating it.

Love. Found. Me.

And now you're all caught up with my love life, sis.

Back to business,

Your Sista

Pause, Reflect, & Discuss

- What about the author's love story intrigues you?

- What do you hope to find out about her journey with Win?

- In what ways do you see your own love story in this letter? (Self-love, family love, romantic love, etc.)

29
That Stomach-Ache Ain't from Too Much Birthday Cake!

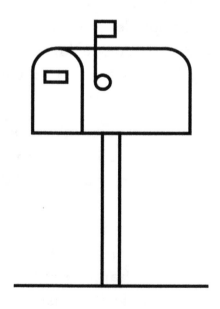

Dear White Woman,

It has been cold and rainy here for over a week! This weather can be god-awful at times, but I didn't let that stop me! Oh no, I went out every day for the last seven days looking for you. But, on day eight the weather really started putting a damper on my search, so I decided to take yesterday off to just rest. I climbed into my king-sized bed with one of my favorite mugs, turned on the Golden Girls and let the tea and the TV rock me to sleep. But don't you know that I would sleep and somehow not rest? Have you ever had that happen? So frustrating!

As I slept, my mind raced all over the place, recalling the highs and lows of this search. I amazed myself thinking about how this search has been going on for decades now, although at times it feels like a lifetime. While many of our siblings have given up on this search to find you, I will not. I refuse. Wrapping my arms around you and healing our souls means more to me than anything in my path that might discourage or deter me from finding you.

Anyways, while I slept, I must have watched a million flashbacks of times when I thought I had encountered you and was wrong. One that stands out so vividly in my mind is my Sweet 16 birthday party. Maybe because as I write this particular letter, we are in the month of April, and maybe not. Nonetheless, we spent so much time together growing up that I ended up at your dad's house most weekends or at your dance competitions supporting you. But something wasn't right, because most times I invited you to come over to my family's house, there was a reason why you couldn't. Until...well, it was my birthday, so you had to come. Right?

You came and there was music, dancing, snacks, games, laughter, and so much more. You seemed to sit off in a corner and not interact with anyone else at the party. Then, right before we cut the cake, you came over to me and whispered in my ear that your dad was coming to pick you up. I was shocked and asked why. You mumbled about how your stomach was aching and walked away.

But it was my birthday for God's sake!

Your dad came, and just like that, you were gone. The girls whispered about you and how they "knew you weren't going to stay" and how they were "shocked that you made it to this side of town." I was devastated. Hurt. Shocked. Betrayed.

As I grow into this work, I am able to look back at my birthday sleepover and to see it differently. Maybe your stomach was indeed hurting. If it was, could it have been the discomfort that you felt being in the racial minority at my party? At school and at your house, you were fine being around me and with me. Was that because you were comfortable in those familiar settings? I'll bet being one of three white people at my party while the other 40 were African American, Latinx, and First Nation/Indigenous made you very uncomfortable. All you had to do was to say, "Hey, sis. I feel so weird being one of the only white people at this party, but damn, you do it every day. I guess it's my turn to step it up." And I would have been there to support you. Ugh! I feel my anger boiling over while writing this because guess what? I was never totally comfortable at your house. Cats on counters, relatives yelling at each other, and no washcloths for God's sake! But did I ever flake out on you? Nope! 'Cause sisters are ride or die.

Waking up from this series of flashbacks made me furious to even think about it, but how could you have known or done any differently? Would you have cared to know or do anything different? I was practicing existing in this same discomfort every day being bussed to your neighborhood school where I was the minority in so many ways. So I was damn good at it. But you, despite all of your awards and intelligence, were a novice at this. In fact, you were one step behind a novice. Know how I know? Because a novice would have at least stayed to sing happy birthday and to open presents, but you had to pull the cord for your parachute to open and to save you.

Isn't it ironic that in the 40 years of practice I've had being in your position, I was never even issued a parachute?

Just food for thought.

Thanking the high heavens I took the day off from this search.

Headed back to sleep,

Your Sista

Pause, Reflect, & Discuss

- What physical symptoms of discomfort have you experienced when in situations where you were in the racial minority? If you've never experienced being in the racial minority, why is that?

- Surely there's been a time, racial difference aside, where you've wanted out. Did you pull the cord to escape that discomfort? Did you use a fake excuse? Or did you tell the truth? How has that escape served you in the short term and done damage in the long term?

30
Sucks Being a Woman, Don't It?

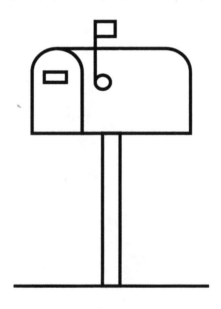

Dear White Woman,

Oh, sis! You have to forgive me! After being admitted to the hospital for more ob/gyn problems, I have decided to take some time off from my search to give my body enough time to recover before I dive back in. I'm not sure if you heard about this wherever you are in the world, but I have the most complicated female system ever.

A few months ago, I was having pain in my ovaries. I thought it was normal period cramping. It wasn't. Then, I thought it was a UTI. It wasn't. Well, after a few tests, they determined it was a dermoid cyst. Given that this thing was squeezing the life out of my ovary (I had the pain to prove it, sis), they decided to remove it. While they were in there, don't you know they found "something weird" in my uterus? So I've been here at the hospital for 48 hours to have yet another surgery to remove what ended up being complex hyperplasia with atypia. This gave me an increased risk of endometrial cancer, so we have been here recovering and waiting on the doctors to come up with the best treatment plan. Fingers crossed! I'm scared out of my mind. I'm either crying or sleeping or a mixture of both. It's awful.

While I knew I had to take some time off after the surgery, that wouldn't stop me before the surgery! I have to tell you that I was looking for you right up until the moment when I was wheeled into the OR. Oh, let me tell you what happened! It was in pre-op that I spotted you. I swear it! You were there! I mean, I never took you for the nursing type, but there you were.

Watching you at the nurses' station and how you kept to yourself, getting your work done, with a quick "hello" here and there, was almost like being in the twilight zone. You wore purple and yellow scrubs and came over to get me prepped for surgery. You greeted me with a smile and a "good morning." You then ran through some instructions to help me get ready. Butterflies stirred in my stomach as I noticed your fingernails. That's how I knew it was you! You have the same fingernails as Mom, the same as Aunt Jean, the same as Grandmother, and the same as me! They were strong and long, and the whites of your nails seemed like you had had a French manicure done. Oh, sis, it was definitely you!

When you returned to see if I had any questions and if I had followed all of your instructions, I caught your eye. I smiled at you, but you looked away. I watched your eyes carefully and sensed an emptiness. Almost as if you were simply going through the motions, and that just couldn't be. Ma always taught us to "do all things heartily, as unto the Lord." But your heart just wasn't in it. I told you I was scared of this surgery, and you responded with a dry "that's normal." You didn't offer any comfort or advice or anything beyond your memorized line of "that's normal."

That's when it hit me. It wasn't you. It couldn't be because the sister I knew was someone who was always overflowing with empathy and compassion. Yes, you kept to yourself and remained focused on your work, but you also knew how to express compassion and empathy for others. You would have said something like, "That's normal, but completely understandable. If I were in this position, I'd be freaked out too. You're brave doing this. You got this."

But you didn't.

As tears ran down my face from the rampant fear and panic flooding my being, you walked away in silence. You literally said nothing. I was wheeled away while passing through this dark emotional cloud of anxiety, and I was alone.

But how could this be? My sister had become a nurse! How could you become a nurse and then not show up when someone needs you? A nurse who doesn't know how to offer care, concern, comfort, compassion, and confidence for ALL patients?

One answer.

It wasn't you.

Yep, that's it.

Couldn't have been.

Longing for your comfort,

Your Sista

Pause, Reflect, & Discuss

- What does care look like in the medical profession to you? Do you expect a different level of care for people you know and love versus random people you don't?

- What was wrong with or missing from the care the nurse gave the author?

- How does the care you extend to people of color, especially women of color, reflect your level of intercultural fluency and cultural competence?

31

I'll Have an Extra-Large Cup of Joy, Please

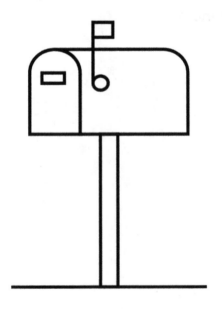

DWW

Dear White Woman,

Hey, sis. So much negativity seems to pour out of television and other media outlets that I needed to take today off to focus on the things that fill me up to overflowing with joy. So I decided to go to the butterfly garden. I rescheduled all my clients and went to fill my joy cup to the top.

I'm smiling as I write this to you. Do you even know what made me fall in love with butterflies, sis? Well, one day years ago now, I was at a stoplight when a butterfly landed on my windshield and hit it too hard. Being the empath that I am, I completely freaked out. I felt awful knowing my car, sitting still at a red light, had killed a butterfly. Well, the light still had not changed because it was one of those intersections in the middle of nowhere on a backroad where the light doesn't ever change. The wind blew the butterfly off my windshield and over into the grass. The empath in me could not rest, so I put my car in park and jumped out to see if I could help this butterfly. *What the hell was I gonna do to help it? Who knows?* As I bent down to see the butterfly, it got up and flew away. Of course, I cried. But more importantly, I decided at that moment that no matter what life brought my way, I wanted to be like that butterfly; I want to be able to get up and to fly away. Always.

That's what I do, sis. No matter what's thrown my way, I get my wings on and I get to flyin'. This happened right after September 11th when I was watching this country regrow her wings.

That's what I'm asking you to do. When I said rock-solid resilience, sis, that's what I meant. That's why I know that no matter how hard it may seem for you to come home, you are strong enough and resilient enough to return to us.

Flying like a butterfly,

Your Sista

Pause, Reflect, & Discuss

- When you feel joy, how do you express it?

- What drains your joy cup? How does that feel?

- What is it that fills your joy cup? How does that feel?

- In what ways has white culture asked you to reject, silence, or ignore your joy? How does this norm minimize the potential growth in your relationships with women of color?

32
She's an Only Pup

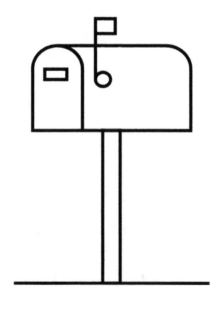

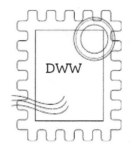

Dear White Woman,

So, I am back at it, sis. I will never give up on my search for you because I know you are out there. I woke up this morning with a renewed commitment to putting this search at the top of my priorities list. While I do have one errand to run today, the rest of my day will be spent following up on new leads on your whereabouts. I'm going to the animal rescue center to see if I can find a little sister for Kwinee. Even saying this out loud makes me sad, as I realize you have never met her. All the smiles and laughter you have missed out on because she is the most hilarious Cavapoo I have ever met.

While pulling into the parking lot, I remembered to leave all the windows cracked so the cool air of the early morning could pass through the truck for Kwin. I brought her with me so she could meet her new little sister too. When I went in, I didn't pay much attention to the other people looking around at the dogs for a new companion.

One of the workers gave me a guided tour and asked me questions about my family structure and preparing for this new addition to our home. While I listened to her, I barely looked at her. I was completely taken by the dogs in the sea of cages around me.

I robotically answered her seemingly routine questions:

"Do you live in a house or an apartment? How many floors? Landlord situation? Rules? Renter's insurance? Number of people in the family? Do you work?" The list of questions went on and on, and then she said it, "Sweetheart," referring to one of the dogs. It sent a jolt through my body. It was someone else's voice when she said that word. In fact, she sounded just like Mom. That's Ma's voice and the way she says, "Hi, sweetheart," when I call her. I then started paying attention to her and every word that came out of her mouth instead of the dogs because I realized it was you! There you were all this time hiding right under my nose at the animal rescue center! The shelter, the pound, or whatever they were calling it these days. How did I not know?

I changed my posture and ruffled through my twists* that I had done two weeks ago and tried to calm my racing thoughts. Should I tell you that it's me? Maybe ask if you remember our first dog, Bootsie? Ughhhh! If you would just slow down and come up for air, I could reveal my identity. You didn't notice the shift in my demeanor at all, but I am now hanging on every syllable that comes out of your mouth! Look at me! Listen to me, to the sound of my voice! And you'll know too!

You rattle on with your questions while the butterflies in my stomach multiply over and over. Then you pause in front of the perfect dog: she is about 10 pounds and is a Shih-Poo. She would be the perfect sister for Kwin, just like you are the perfect sister for me. You ask as you look over her chart, "Which shelter did Kwin come from?" as if you knew beyond a shadow of a doubt that Kwin was also a rescue. I found my footing enough to answer that Kwin came from an Amish family living on a farm where they breed Cavapoos. Silly me.

Something in you shifted as you asked, "Wait, Kwin isn't a rescue?" Your tone was different.

It was suddenly dark, deep, and judgmental. You started talking about all your rescue dogs at home, as if they were a badge of honor. You abruptly lost interest in knowing anything else about Kwin, as if she was less precious because she came from a breeder. I mean, I know you are into animal rights and rescue animals, but your demeanor changed in a way that signaled to me you didn't approve of our breeder-purchased dog. What was so bad about buying a puppy from a litter on a farm? And how did picking one from a rescue center make you better than me?

Needless to say, I did exactly what Ma had always trained us to do. With the poor customer service you were giving me suddenly, I decided that my money would not be spent here at your shelter. I interrupted your judgmental line of questions with, "Thanks for your help, but I'll just contact the breeder to see if they have any new litters." And with that, I left.

Don't worry, I knew that woman could not have been you. You would never judge anyone for how they brought a dog into their family. No more than you would judge someone for buying a shirt from the mall instead of traveling to the village across the world where it was made to help the family living in poverty. I will tell you I am furious! How dare she judge me?!

I know it wasn't you.

You would never behave like that. Even if it was a simple and slight change in tone, it was piercing and cut deep.

Thank God Ma raised us differently.

I love you, sis.

As soon as I drop Kwin, the dog from the litter on the Amish farm, at home, I will resume my search.

With love despite your judgment,

Your Sista

---

*Twists – a hairstyle, short for two-strand twists. This is where you take a small section of hair, divide it into two strands and wrap one around the other. Don't worry, sis; it's cute!

Pause, Reflect, & Discuss

- What white standard or cultural norm have you imposed on someone else when it comes to adopting/owning pets? (Before you say none, this includes, but is not limited to: only adopting from a shelter, letting cats climb all over everything, letting your pets sleep in the bed with you, leaving all your pet's hair all over your vehicle, never crating your animal, etc.)

- If owning a pet does not apply to you or any of your family members, what white standard or cultural norm in general have you used to judge others? Are you aware of the cultural norms of whiteness? If not, why not?

33
Fireworks and Lightning

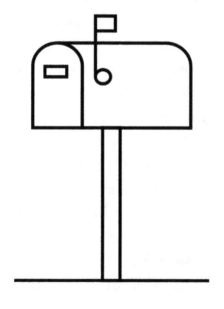

Dear White Woman,

Hey, sis. I know I begin lots of my letters to you like that, but don't you remember whenever we saw each other we'd always say "Hey, sis"? Anyways, I let our mother convince me to go to the Fourth of July celebration on the beach down here in South Carolina. I didn't plan to go because the weather forecast was just nasty—storms, storms, and more storms. Who wants that? I gave in and went, and boy did I have a headache by the end of the night. You know I've had migraines since I was 15 years old. And, as I've gotten older, I have different triggers. Flashing lights and direct sunlight are guarantees for a migraine. It's been so bad at times, the doctors had to give me stronger medicine for when over-the-counter migraine medications weren't working. Now, sis, I know that talking about illness is considered too private, or a sign of weakness, according to the rules of whiteness, but if we're gonna be sisters, we need to be able to talk about this stuff. Hell, we may even be able to heal one another.

We miraculously found parking pretty close to the concert stage and headed for a restaurant that makes every burger you can imagine. This way we could see the concert stage and the fireworks without actually stepping foot on the sand. I thought I would take the day off from searching for you, but I changed my mind once I got up onto the restaurant's balcony. I looked out and saw a sea of faces, and they all looked like you. Just like you, sis! But one person stood out in particular, and I was determined to confirm that it was you. I was so sure of it that I wanted to tear down your posters all over town and to bring you to the family reunion we've been waiting for.

As we approached our booth, this woman stared at me from a distance but would not break her gaze. She watched me from the moment we stepped foot on the property. I stared back looking for familiarity in her face. While I didn't immediately see it, I thought maybe you recognized me this time. So as I got closer, I watched her face turn to a very puzzled look, and she gave this same look to Ma, Win, our cousin, and our niece. Once we climbed the stairs and were seated on the balcony, I looked out and saw her still looking at us. And then I saw it. The white gaze*.

She didn't recognize me. She wasn't my long-lost sister. I guess our presence threw her off. It was only after we were seated at our table that I realized we were literally the sole Black family at the celebration.

I should have just stayed home.

That's all.

Am I searching in vain?

So fucking exhausted,

Your Sista

*The white gaze – when a white person stares at you like they are shocked to see you in the same space as them, they are wondering what you are doing near them, or they experience a subconscious moment of cognitive dissonance because a person of color is in a space that their subconscious mind has deemed for "whites only." No, you don't do this intentionally. Nor do you think or wonder these things on a conscious level. *Deep breaths.* Still having trouble believing this? Look it up.

Pause, Reflect, & Discuss

- When was the last time you were stared at because you didn't belong? Describe this incident. Describe how it felt.

- When was the last time you stared at someone because they didn't belong? Describe this incident. Remember, "not belonging" is a synonym for someone or something different from "the norm," someone with a disability, wearing "un-American" attire, Black or brown, "too" tall, "too" short, "too" curvy, etc. How did it feel to find yourself staring?

- Where might the family go next year instead of that beach for holiday celebrations? Does this bother or affect you somehow?

- What messages did you get about talking/showing illness in your home culture?

34
Bring Me Back
a Keychain

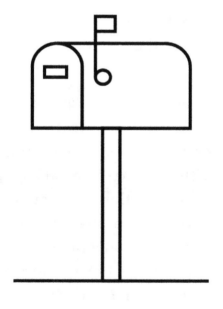

Dear White Woman,

Hey, sis! I am still here in Myrtle Beach. I'm trying to soak up every bit of vacation I can before I go back to being called on at any moment of any day. While I am soaking in some much-needed warmth from the sun, I have been showing Win and her mom the touristy things to do here. We went to this amazing outdoor mall that has only grown bigger and better over the years called Blackberries at the Beach this morning, and we went early to beat the crowds and the sun. It can get so hot down here!

While there were many things we did, ate, and saw while we were there, passing through one souvenir shop in particular really stopped me in my tracks. With my part-time Latinx upbringing, you know I love all things from the Spanish-speaking world. So you already know I was so excited to be in the souvenir shop with hand-made souvenirs from all over Latin America. In fact, even the name made me feel good inside—

Hers and Mayans. Such a cute name for such a cute place. There were so many colors, statues, bags, jewelry, and so much more! You probably needed to come to this place two or three times to be able to take in all it had to offer.

We got there pretty soon after it opened, and people seemed to be almost sleepwalking. As we walked around the shop, I noticed the owner of the shop had on a shirt that looked a lot like a shirt we both had as young girls. It was a purple shirt with yellow writing that said "Don't worry" on the front and "Be happy" on the back. This was our shirt! I swore we were the only two on the planet to be wearing this as anything other than a night shirt to sleep in. Who else would go out in this hideous thing? It had to be you! I had found you early in the morning at Blackberries! I wasn't even looking for you! No offense, sis, but it was too early in the morning to be focused on my search.

I did everything I could to get a closer look at you, and finally we worked our way around the shop to the side where you were. You were standing near the front counter with your hands behind your back as if you were waiting to complete a sale. As we approached you, I could smell the shampoo and perfume that you always wore in school. Another confirmation that it was you! Nobody else on the planet used the stuff! As we got closer, you gave me a look, and I was confused. Then you gave my Win the same look, and she felt confused.

Then your face changed to a welcoming one.

It was when you saw Win's mom.

My future mother-in-law.

My white future mother-in-law.

Then it all made sense, and we were no longer confused. What we saw in your face when you saw Win's mom was affinity. You saw someone who looked like you and dressed like you. Her presence made you more comfortable. You felt relaxed and reassured, safe around her. Nothing wrong with this, sis. Just learn how to manage your biases and be more welcoming to those with whom you don't share affinity.

Anyways, we were certain and sure.

Certain and sure that it was not you.

I love you, sis. And I know Ma raised us better than this. I know it wasn't you, but I had hoped it was. I'll get back to it tomorrow. I'm just tired, you know?

Still loving you,

Your Sista

Pause, Reflect, & Discuss

- What is white solidarity? How does it show up in your life?

- What did the owner of the shop see when she looked at the author and her partner? What did she see when she looked at the white woman who was the author's future mother-in-law?

- Do you have strategies for managing your biases?

35
Each One,
Reach One,
and Teach One

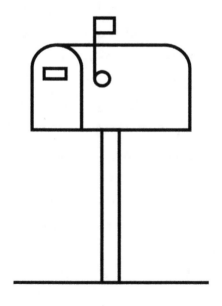

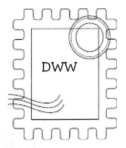

Dear White Woman,

I'm writing you with just one preparation that you can make for your return home. I know! I know! What about the search?! I'll get back to that in a minute. Sis, here's my advice: get a coach! And find a community! I may not have time to write you as many letters as I would like before you come home, and I want you to be ready.

Maybe you're confused by what I wrote here. What I mean is to look up DEI coaches and consultants who coach clients one-on-one or in small groups to really help you to move your personal journey forward. A coach can help you with this, sis. While there are some open slots in my practice, there aren't many with all the traveling I do. It doesn't mean you have to meet each week or even every two weeks; you just have to start somewhere. Sis, some of my clients only meet with me once a month, and that's enough for them to feel the progress they want to see in their own lives.

The other thing that's gone really well for my clients is joining a local antiracist community like AWARE LA or CCI Boston or SURJ. You gotta work on that "I'm an individual" bullshit if you're actually committed to this journey home. Community is KEY for all y'all white folks! I'll tell you this: when you do come home, there gonna be some rough moments, and you're gonna want to talk about them. This community is where the white people who can help you through those rough patches are gonna be. 'Cause you can't keep asking me to sort through and do your dirty laundry.

After you've been in practice for a while, start helping your other sisters to prepare to come home. Be patient with them. They are learning just like you. They will make mistakes and forget what you've taught them, and that's okay. You're going to keep making mistakes too. You're working against years and decades, even centuries, of training and conditioning to help yourself and them unlearn cultural norms and practices.

Be patient.

Express empathy.

Call them in. Not out.

Just think, sis, if each one did indeed reach one and teach just one more white sister, how much further along we'd all be.

Just a thought.

Now, go get a coach and a community!

Love you sis,

Your Sista

P.S. Don't forget your laundry boo.

Pause, Reflect, & Discuss

- Are you working with a coach and/or in community to get better at issues surrounding race, racism, and whiteness (a.k.a. your dirty laundry)?

- What about working with a coach or joining an antiracist community gives you pause or hesitation?

- Are you able to empathize with white women who are not as far along as you? What does that empathy look like in real time?

36
Am I On
Mute?

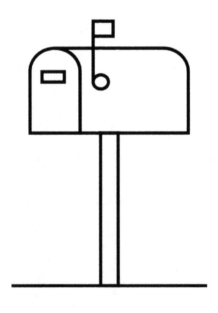

Dear White Woman,

Well, they finally gave me a seat at the table. They have put me in a position on the Senior Admin Team, and I have spent the last few days in something called the Admin Retreat, where each day of meetings ends with a nice meal. We learn and discuss a great deal, and there is even some arguing over decisions that need to be made about how we will proceed as we move into the school year. It can be intense, fun, and boring all at the same time.

As new members of the team, we have been encouraged to speak up and make our voices heard. So I set out to do just that. If something resonated with me, I spoke up and echoed the sentiments with examples. If I disagreed, I spoke up and shared examples to support my opinions. Well, as I shared a disagreement, I noticed one lady staring at me. She was almost staring through me, as if she was there but wasn't there at the same time. She had that glazed-over look that said she might be hungry and was tired of being in that meeting.

As I looked back at her, I noticed her earrings. They were radiant! These beautiful silver earrings dangled above her shoulders and kind of moved back and forth as her head moved around. They were gorgeous, and you *know* how much I love earrings. I'm practically addicted to them, sis! Just two years ago when we were thinking about what we would do to celebrate my 40th birthday, I asked Win to buy me 40 pairs of earrings. That's pretty much an earring addiction. But now I'm wondering if I'm like this because Ma never let us leave the house without earrings on. Huh...weird. Oh, well...it's a great addiction to have.

Anyways, back to those silver earrings! I realized that no one else on earth would pick out a pair of silver earrings as unique as those. The yellow and purple accents on them reminded me of the hippy feel we like getting from our clothes, shoes, and jewelry. Remember that store at the mall in Myrtle Beach? These earrings must have come from there! When I was there I kept thinking, how does this store stay open? How many people on the planet are there who like this kind of stuff? And guess who I thought of? You! Which only meant one thing, sis. You were here at this very table! You must have accepted the most recently open position while I was away on vacation! It was you! Of course! I know that glazed-over look anywhere!

While my heart knew it was you, what really confirmed it was how you said, "Thanks, Kim," after each comment I made. I felt so validated and seen! It was like sisters against the world all over again. How would I let you know it wasn't just "Kim," but it was me! It was your sista! How would I reveal myself to you? I sat quietly thinking about it, planning it out carefully. Joyfully. Giddy almost, sis!

Just when I thought I was ready, I heard your response to my co-director's comments. You responded with, "Excellent point! I am so glad you brought that up! I was hoping someone would say this! Brilliant." I was taken aback because he was saying all the same things I was saying, yet he was somehow more exciting. I was puzzled, confused, and felt rejected all at the same time. Why was I left with a "thanks, Kim," and he received accolades upon accolades for his "brilliant" ideas? That were mine.

Wait....I remember reading about this phenomenon. There was a book that touched on this. What was the name of it?

Ah, *Why Black Men Love White Women*....That's it! It was happening right in front of my eyes! Somehow, what a man of color was saying was so much more valuable than when it came out of a woman of color's mouth. With white women as the standard of beauty, the standard of excellence, and the standard of all things desirable, it sets women of color, especially Black women, up for failure. This man of color became this exotic and desirable being in that meeting and was worshipped. I know, sis, you want to attribute it to the patriarchy, but this is different. Look up that book, sis, and read it.

Anyway, that's when I was let down.

I knew my sister would not put any bond above the one we shared as sisters. You would never uplift this man and not also lift up your sista with equal amounts of recognition and praise.

Never. It wasn't you.

Maybe you had sold those earrings to a consignment shop and someone else bought them. Because those were definitely your earrings.

Disappointed,

Your Sista

Pause, Reflect, & Discuss

- In what ways do you support "the patriarchy" even if it means fighting against rights and policies for women? More specifically, in what ways are you supporting that patriarchy against your sistas of color in everyday situations like the one above?

- In what ways has the patriarchy worked against you even though you've supported it?

- Can you see how women divided across racial, ability, class, sexual orientation, gender fluidity, and other lines hold the patriarchy in place?

37
One Planet, Two Pandemics

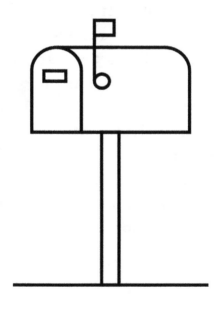

Dear White Woman,

Oh, sis. Oh, sis. Oh, sis! I am typing this letter through so many tears. I can barely see what I'm writing. I can feel it! I am so close to finding you! I know it in my soul that I'm almost there. But, now, the world is shutting down!

So much is happening. I am speechless and so broken-hearted. There's a virus headed our way that is killing people left and right. Something about us being "due for another one," since 100 years have passed since the last one. Sis, they can't figure out how it is spreading, and people just keep dropping dead all around us. So many people are dying. Their best guess is that it is airborne and passed through touch. We've started wearing masks and gloves everywhere we go. And where are we going? Nowhere. Everyone is mandated to stay at home.

The day before this global crisis was announced,

I had to have an emergency hysterectomy. That's right, my tumultuous ob/gyn journey has come to an end because I couldn't stop bleeding. So, I've been home recovering from yet another surgery (I know, I know. The doctors say I need a frequent flyer card LOL!), and I hold my breath every time Win leaves the house for food, water, and toilet paper. Toilet paper, sis....Folks have started hoarding toilet paper! And all the while, people are dying everywhere—all over the world. Everyone has either lost someone to this virus or knows someone who lost someone. It seems that we are stuck in a perpetual state of panic, fear, and depression.

While people are worried about contracting this illness and dying or losing loved ones, the entire world is witnessing what seems like the unveiling of a racial pandemic at the same time. Sis, we watched angry white men hunt down Ahmaud Arbery and kill him like he was a rabid dog. We watched cops shoot 32 bullets through Breonna Taylor's apartment, killing her and arresting her boyfriend. She was an EMT...trained to save people...to work with the police. Sis, the person they were looking for wasn't even there! Like, how does that happen?! How do you explain that?! And then, just when we couldn't bear any more, or thought we couldn't, the entire world watched George Floyd get murdered by a white police officer kneeling for nine minutes and 29 seconds on his neck. Oh, sis, this is leading to worldwide protests in parts of the world where I didn't even know they cared about the plight of the Black American.

Being an empath, all of this sunk me pretty low. I am crying daily. My life has become recovering, crying, and sleeping. My search has to be suspended. I am tending to myself, Win, and Kwinee of course.

During this time, I have also made peace with the fact that I must abandon my search here because we are moving to the west coast where we accepted new job offers. Maybe I'll find you out west, but how if we are on lockdown? We aren't allowed to go anywhere that isn't deemed "necessary." We are traveling across the country without stopping to rest. We plan to switch drivers back and forth until we reach our destination, only stopping for gas. We packed food and water and are determined not to catch this virus. We will make it safely and hunker down, sis. We are scared out of our minds.

We are scared to die of COVID-19.

We are scared to die of being Black.

We are scared of white people, sis. They are coming undone. And they are scared of us. Everyone is on eggshells.

And the election is fast approaching. The entire world has eyes on this country that seems to be falling apart more and more each day.

We stay home for fear of being harmed. We order groceries online for fear of contracting COVID-19. I just can't search for you during this time. So much has been put on pause without our consent that I decided we couldn't wait anymore. I chose what would happen next.

As I sit and reflect now, I can't help but to share this:

I knew I loved Win, and I wanted to marry her. So, one morning, we spent time dancing to Alicia Keys' song "Like

You'll Never See Me Again." We danced and danced and cried and cried. All at the same time. I knew we both felt the fragility and uncertainty of our existence on this planet. We silently thought about the idea of losing each other to this COVID-19 virus or to the virus of anti-Blackness, and we wept in each other's arms.

I decided then.

Later that morning as Win went to hang a picture on the wall, I texted family and friends to get on Facebook live in a few minutes. I logged on and positioned the phone so everyone could watch what was happening. I read the lyrics from the song we had danced to earlier, and then I said, "So, if all of this is true, can I ask you a question?" She replied, "Yeah, what's wrong?" I responded, "If I asked you to marry me, would you?" She answered, "Of course I would." So I pulled out her ring, opened the box, and said, "Well, will you marry me?" She said yes in front of our family and friends from all over the world, lol. It was such a beautiful moment, and it was something we felt we could take control over. In that moment we weren't afraid.

We had each other.

And we were enough.

We still have each other.

Hoping you're okay,

Your Sista

Pause, Reflect, & Discuss

- How intense were your fears for yourself and your family during the pandemic? What kinds of things were scaring you the most?

- Have you ever felt that same level of fear for yourself and your family because of your race?

- How has chronic fear impacted your health, spirit, and wellness?

38
Who's Karen?

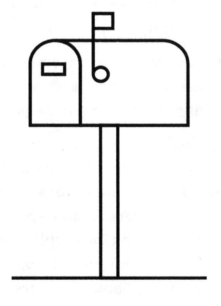

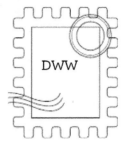

DWW

Dear White Woman,

So as some restrictions are being lifted, people are out and about. We are living our lives in a very weird way. We are wearing masks everywhere we go. We are going to work and wearing masks. We are watching the death toll climb and praying it's no one we know.

Well, sis, some of those people are indeed people we knew. We lost two individuals who were friends of the family.

While we grieved those losses, we couldn't grieve like we needed to because a wave of imposters started showing up claiming to be you, sis.

Maybe they had heard about the search, but they were frauds. The world started calling them "Karens" because they are always carin' 'bout the wrong thing. They were falling apart, sis. They were white women going into public places saying things like, "Give us our country back," and "I'll call the police on you," and they were! They were calling the police on Black and brown people for doing normal things like having a barbecue or birdwatching! They were laying on the ground screaming, kicking, and crying claiming someone was attacking them! They were calling the police for people showing up to rental properties on vacation or even going to their own homes. For people asking them to wear masks. For people asking them to leash their dog in public. For people taking naps. For people not cleaning snow off their cars. For selling bottled water. For people "stealing their cell phone" although they hadn't—and so much more, sis. The list goes on. And on. And on.

I knew in my heart that none of these Karens could be you because we were not raised like that. We value humanity over anything else, sis. Don't you remember? I know you do! This is just foolishness. I have started searching for you from a distance because I can't end up in a situation where someone calls the cops on me for saying good morning to them. I just can't risk it, sis. Black people end up dead for these sorts of things. I wanna live.

I wanna live.

So please come home.

Love,

Your Sista

Pause, Reflect, & Discuss

- What do you know about the terms Karen or Becky? How does it feel knowing that even when you do your work, women of color who don't know you still have to assume you're a Karen or Becky? Our survival as women of color may depend on that very assumption.

- Have you ever shown up as a Karen or Becky?

- How has the Karen/Becky legacy made women of color more hesitant to trust you, or even be in your presence?

39
So Close

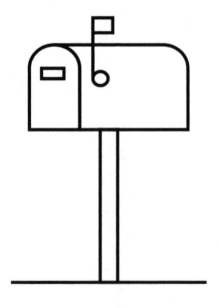

Dear White Woman,

Oh sis, I told you! I told you I'm feeling close. I woke up today, and the pandemic be damned. I feel you nearby. I can't explain it, but it's in the air. All the sadness and tears have been worth it. I can just feel it. Take it from this empath, I feel your presence. I don't know how, and I don't know when, but I can feel you.

I'm smiling as I write you this letter because I know it in my gut. I'm also crying because I'm overflowing with anxious joy as I write. I know you are close, sis. I'm so nervous! How do I set up your room? Will you want to stay with me? Ugh.... What if you don't understand the way I talk? What if you hate gay people? What if Kwin doesn't like you? Eh, Kwin *likes everyone.* What if you don't like Win? No, of course you'll like her!

So many preparations... *Wait, but wait. Deep breaths.* Have I told you everything you need to know before you come home? Definitely not. That's okay. I'll help you get used to being back at home. It won't be roses every day, but I'm committed to you and to our sisterhood. There's only one rule:

Promise me that you will be open to me sharing when you are bringing the kidnapper's ways home. That way we can work through where that behavior comes from, why it's offensive, and what we can do to heal and to move forward as sisters.

Can you promise me that, sis? With you being so close, I need you to promise me that.

I need that or don't come home. I know that's harsh, but I have a sisterhood already with all of the women you left behind. And I cannot betray their trust and safety. I just won't.

So promise me, sis.

So close,

Your Sista

Pause, Reflect, & Discuss

- What else do you think you need to know before you come home?

- Are you able to make the commitment that the author asks of you?

- Can you name three things that you must do before coming home? Do you have a white partner, or a larger white community, to work with on this so you don't feel so alone? And so you get it done?! #Accountability

40
Finally, You
Found Me

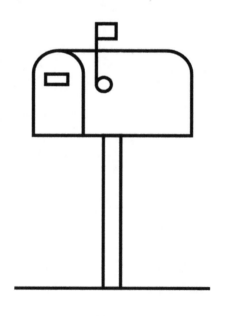

Dear White Woman,

Sis! So much has happened since I last wrote to you. Let's see!

- Win and I are planning our wedding. We also bought our first home, and we love it. She is also writing her first book!

- Kwinee now has a little sister named Mari (like the word for butterfly in Spanish: Mariposa).

- And COVID-19 literally changed *the whole* of this earth, and there is so much death all around us.

While we celebrate some things, and despite others, here we are holding joy and pain at the same time with vaccines in our arms. Sometimes the masks are on, and sometimes they aren't. Regardless, we have continued to search for you. Spotting you behind a mask has been even more difficult, so today I'm executing my newest plan.

I'm returning to look for you, one last time, in

a place we often called home. Home is where the heart, the mind, the body, and the soul all feel safe. For us, that has always been the bookstore, a library, or a book fair. I'm passing through our favorite aisles (mysteries, self-help, autobiographies, and imaginative social justice non-fiction) to check just one more time. Hearing complete silence means that most shoppers are engrossed in whatever book they are skimming, but that won't deter me. As I pass through the aisles, I begin to smile as I feel your presence. I've got butterflies again!

Wait! There?! With my book in her hands!

Is that? Wait!

With papers and writing pads all around with notes on them?

Tears are filling my eyes. Is that my book?! Yes! It is! My book has colorful tabs marking important pages to remember. My heart is literally pounding; she's doing the work!

Is that? Wait.

Just look up for one second!

Oh.

My.

God.

It is you! You were here all this time? Doing exactly what any sister of mine would be doing. The work to prepare to come home!

Welcome home, sis! Oh my God! I can't believe this moment is finally here!

I am filled with so much joy and so many questions for you! But I can't stop hugging you! I don't wanna let you go! I'm so afraid you'll leave us again.

Sis, all this time, I should have come back here, because you clearly had an active role in this investigation. But I thought you had forgotten about our bond.

Our relationship.

Our friendship.

Our sisterhood.

And here, today, in my arms with faces soaked with tears, is my reward.

You have finally come home.

Here, in your hands, you hold my pain and my joy, my exhaustion and my energy, my confusion and my clarity, my weakness and my strength, my humanity and my vulnerability. You hold all of it, sis. Because this entire time, you too, have been searching for me.

Welcome home.

Love always,

Your Sista

Pause, Reflect, & Discuss

- What plan of action will you take now that you have finished reading this book?

- What steps will you take to heal relationships with women of color in your life?

- How can I be sure it's you next time I think I've spotted you?

For White Women Who've Made it this Far

Thank you for taking this journey of healing and connection with me. Thank you for crying with me, for laughing with me, and for getting angry enough to do something. Thank you for buying this book and for passing it on. Thank you for gifting it to other people you know. Thank you for your vulnerability. Thank you for your willingness to learn. Thank you for holding these memories and stories in all of their fragility and for responding with love, care, and action.

Now that you know better, thank you for doing better. Thank you for pushing yourself to answer the end-of-chapter questions. Thank you for dropping and abandoning your weapons of defensiveness, distance, and silence. Thank you for reaching out to sisters of color to heal the wounds you have caused. Thank you for reaching out to coaches and working within a community to get help with your journey towards cultural competence and building an anti-racist lifestyle.

Thank you for your dissatisfaction with where you are and your determination to grow and to be transformed. Thank you for showing up for yourself and for your sistas by using your voice, agency, and access where women of color cannot. Thank you.

Thank you for understanding how broken our sisterhood is and for your desire to mend it. Thank you for apologizing when you mess up and for leaving the excuses, explanations, and your lists of good intentions out of it. Thank you for debriefing your mistakes with your white sisters and honoring your commitment to doing better.

Thank you for being here in this space with me.

With gratitude and humility,

Your sista, Kimberlee Yolanda Williams

Acknowledgements

I have to say that sitting down with these acknowledgements excited me and terrified me all at the same time. I'm excited because thinking of how all of you (or most of you) have supported me throughout this process fills up my joy cup. Terrified because I'm so afraid of forgetting someone. So, here goes nothing.

To all of the people who listened to me and didn't tell me I was crazy for wanting to write this book, thank you. Your belief in me and in this project sustained me when I wasn't sure I could reach the finish line.

To the people who told me I was crazy and shouldn't do it, thank you. It was your doubt and your advice to go after low hanging fruit that pushed me when I lost steam and was too tired to get through.

To my mom, for reading the manuscript, getting angry, traveling down memory lane with more of your stories, sharing feedback, and for teaching me so many of the life lessons shared in this book, thank you, and I love you!

To my family for supporting me throughout this process, thank you! To Joi Lynn (who will say that's not her real name), thank you for weighing in on the cover. To Bobo (who will also say that's not his real name), thank you for always answering when I call you crying. To Mijo (who actually will also say that's not his real name), thank you for our weekly chats. To our niece, Shieyenne, thank you for joining our family in the final stage of this project and for making our home feel even more complete. Thank you for family dinners, family reading time, family question time, family journal time, and family gym time. And, yes!, your cooking is on point, too!

To the readers in the focus groups who were among the first to lay eyes on this project: Shea Fleming, Vanessa Rojas, Martha Kiley, Jania Hoover, Lucia Kittredge, Emily Hummel, Kisha Palmer, Michelle Chalmers, Claire Tuttle, Kathryn Rosenberg, Carolyn Lackey, and Jamie Crouse Thank you for your questions, your pushback, your emotions, and your willingness to sit with my manuscript in her infancy.

To all of my sistas who validated these stories with your own stories and let me borrow them for this book, your tears, your laughter, and your "chileeeeeeee please" held me down. I could not have done this without you pushing and encouraging me. When I wanted to give up because I was experiencing new encounters with white women and losing faith during this process, you held space for me and never let me quit.

To the white women who showed up everywhere I looked on this journey giving me just one more letter to write, thank you. That sounds shady as hell, but it's so true! Thank you for reaffirming the need for the gift of my book to the world.

To the white women who are doing the work so much that they are standing against racism on days where I'm too tired to stand at all, I say thank you.

To Maggie, thank you for helping me to see the value in my work so long ago, for helping push the project in its final stage, and for asking me to show up more authentically in our interactions. You are enough.

To my publisher, my sister, and my friend, Debby, whew! To think this all began around nasty ass salads with lettuce as the one and only ingredient. Do you remember that?! Ugh, disgusting! But, actually it truly began after Win bought us tickets to you and Faith English's event (BLACK & WHITE WOMEN: Reconciling Our Past, Re-Defining Our Future) for my birthday. Not sure we ever even had the chance to discuss the inspiration for the book. For seeing the need for this book, for pushing my authentic voice when I went a bit too white, for challenging me to think bigger, for troubleshooting with me when I couldn't figure things out, for taking my texts that came in at the wrong time, for anchoring me every step of the way, for asking me to tell you the unfiltered truth and for making space for it, for owning your whiteness when it showed up, for making the publishing journey memorable in every way, and for being my sister. I say thank you! Bonus track-Thanks for letting me borrow Bruce for that last round of editing!

To my editor, Shaundale, lawd! You were like a breath of fresh air! Meeting with you felt like coming home for a family reunion every single time! You pushed me and challenged me even when I thought I was already done. You officially convinced me that I use the words sis and that wayyyyy too much, lol. Your passion for my project made me believe even more deeply in it. The things you asked me to interrogate and to wrestle with took me to new and undiscovered places in my heart. You were such a resource beyond the editing process, too! Every writer should have you in their corner!

To my formatter, Ebony Rose, of Ignited Ink 717 your energy makes me believe anything is possible. You took the pages of my manuscript and breathed life into my vision. You are so good at what you do! Even when I didn't know the words to use to describe what I was seeing, you took that and ran with it. You da realest! Thank you!

To my cover designer, Brad. Wow, wow, and wow! I wanted to be in love with the cover, and I am! Thank you for making my cover call to the readers it was designed to reach. I could not have imagined that the cover of my book would bring tears to MY eyes and take my breath away like it has! It's certainly been a journey to creating the right one. Thank you!

To my colleagues who listened to me read letters and cried, laughed, and sat in silence with me, thank you!

To the DEI directors from all over this country who have supported me along this journey, thank you for who you are in my life.

To my brothas who hold me down and answer whenever I call: Ray, Bobo, Mijo, Percy, and Bertrand. Thank you for all of our chats, your encouragement, your faith in me, and your support.

To the tribe of women who hold me down with random texts, calls, emails, lunches, spa days, laughs, hugs, cards, "I'm thinking about you" gifts, weekend desserts, and gummies (Albanese only, of course. Thanks to Jania for that!): Nyasia, Shelly, Monay, Lydia, Happy, Momma Linda, Jo, Carla, Arnika, Valerie, Nanette, and Vanessa-mujer!. Thank you for always looking out for me, challenging me to be better, demanding that I take care of myself and put myself first, and for loving me for who I am.

To Joslyn, thank you for jumping in the fire with me no matter how hot it is. You literally get me from point A to point B every day without complaining about how busy my life is. You consistently push me to be a better me, by seeing the light that I carry inside me even when I can't see my way in the darkness. You protect me when others seek to violate my boundaries (including me). Our laughs, chats, and even freakouts when my schedule abruptly changes are the best lol. You are the engine that gets me from Monday morning to Friday evening in one piece and at peace. I couldn't have done this without you. Thank you!

To my counselor, thank you for walking me through the valleys of sadness and brokenness along this journey. For helping me to access the power and resilience of my ancestors in order to heal from each and every microaggression and story revealed in this book. For helping me to find joy in bringing this gift to the world while processing all the pain it brought up. For helping me to learn and to clearly see what does and does not belong to me. For teaching me to see just how worthy I am, and simply because I exist, thank you. For showing me how to return to my body and to ground myself when my inner empath takes over, thank you. For teaching me to celebrate myself, to laugh harder, to resist by resting, and for so much more, I say thank you!

To those who, no matter how hard I tried, I forgot to mention. Thank you for who you are to me and how you show up in my life. I love you.

To my rock, Win, you are my smile and my strength. You believed me when we came home from that workshop and I told you I'd write this book, even though I kinda thought I was joking. You trusted me to tell the truth and to write it in a way that it would bridge gaping divides. You held me when the letters sunk me to dark and sad places that wounded me. You shared your own stories again and again even though they made you cry. You listened to each new letter and held pain and doubt alongside hope and healing. You held my hand when I sat in the car crying about this project. You sang Backstreet Boys songs to me when I needed a good laugh. You loved me when life made me feel like love was impossible. You gave me the strength to cross the finish line.

I'm so lucky and blessed to love you and to be loved by you. You have shared me with countless others, and yet, you make me feel like it's just the two of us. And, yes, we are enough. Thank you!

About the Author

Hailing from the nation's capital with huge hair, a million-watt smile, and contagious laughter, Kimberlee Yolanda Williams has had a heart for the perceived underdog for as long as she can remember. From her earliest years, Kimberlee's experiences unfolded in communities filled with diversity of every kind, where gatherings around topics of equity and inclusion were explored with courageous authenticity. She grew up thinking engaging across differences was something everyone wanted to do and knew how to do. So why didn't they do it?

As an educator, DEI administrator, consultant, workshop leader, speaker, and certified life and health coach, she has found herself in a variety of U.S. cities. With each new context she increasingly understood what held people back from crossing social divisions. Kimberlee found herself able to consciously place herself in the center of these divisions, in particular racial dynamics, and support people across the racial spectrum in stepping closer to one another.

Kimberlee is first and foremost a humanist, a deep believer in what is possible when humanity is centered. Her mix of authenticity and raw truth gives permission for those around her to choose progress over perfection and bring their full selves into the room. She is known for finding humor and challenge at just the right moments, and like the best of coaches, leaning in and pushing audiences just enough to believe in the potential she sees. Her approach of connection and compassion is what makes a consultation feel like a conversation with your best friend, a workshop feel like a workout with your favorite trainer, and a presentation feel like a present from your closest confidant.

Kimberlee received a B.A. in Foreign Language Education from the University of Maryland (go Terps!) and an M.S. in Education from Dominican University. She currently lives in Seattle with her partner, where they refuel by being in community (with other folks of color), reading and reading some more, and relaxing near any body of water. In addition to all of the above, Kimberlee is a daughter, a granddaughter, a sister, a cousin, an aunt, a niece, a dancer, an avid learner of languages (five to date), a free spirit, an empath, and now a writer.

Dear White Woman, Please Come Home is Kimberlee's attempt to share with readers what her clients, workshop attendees, and audience members have felt for years. She always brings her full self, her DC flare, her sass, and her humor. She's the best friend you didn't know you had.

Learn more about and follow Kimberlee at her website engagingacrossdifference.com.

CPSIA information can be obtained
at www.ICGtesting.com
Printed in the USA
LVHW021251090222
710594LV00010BA/1140